First published in the UK in 2000 by Feather Books
before the present publishing company
Revised edition published in 2017 by

Inspire & Bless Ltd ®

35 St Pauls Drive, Wellington,
Telford, Shropshire, England, TF1 3GD
www.inspireandbless.co.uk

hyadjepong@inspireandbless.co.uk

ISBN 978-1-909094-15-4

i

# TESTIMONIALS

*"Hannah's poems are thought provoking whilst touching you directly in a way that opens your heart to experience the depth of human emotion — both joy and pain."*

Darshana Ubl - Investor and SME Advisor

*"Having known Hannah in the few years we spent in Bridgend, her poetry brings back memories of her contributions in the fellowship there.*
*"Her reminiscences of life experiences shine through with such vivid expression that the reader can`t help but be transported to a different world - a world where spiritual values excel."*

Rev. Tom Stables — Retired pastor of Apostolic Church, Bridgend

*"There are milestones in the progression of every poet's craft – writing a first poem, first giving a reading, and for a talented few, being published.*

*However, some poets have the special gift to reach our hearts on the deepest level. For this reason these poets deserve extra recognition. This elite group earns our attention, our gratitude and our praise."*

International Library of Poetry
and the International Society of Poets

This revised edition is dedicated to my husband
Mr Samuel Ellis Adjepong.

Your interest and pride in my work has been a
great encouragement. Thank you for the laptop,
tablet and smartphones I use as devices to
compose my poems.

Thank you also for the many nights you listened
patiently as I read another poem to you.
I appreciate your comments and compliments.

*Hannah*

# CONTENTS

# ACKNOWLEDGEMENTS

I am thankful to all the dedicated teachers whose passion was to see their pupils excel. I would like to mention the late Mr. C. B. Donkor, and Mr. Bawonke, who were very passionate and made school an amazing place to learn. Mr. Apraku was not only a great teacher but was also an officer in the Young Pioneer movement. The discipline of that movement helped me to think differently.

Mrs. Theresa Ayaovi Senoo, headmistress of GBI Central RC Girls School was so passionate about poetry that she made learning and reciting a great joy. She also helped me, through her affirmation and compliments, to love poetry. I called her two years ago to ask permission to mention her name in my book. She could not put a face to my name but when I started reciting *Bishop Hatto*, she immediately responded. I am grateful that I am able to honour your passion for poetry this way.

To the late Mr. Kwame Oforochen, my cousin who also loved to recite poetry; our times together at Takoradi will never be forgotten. Your love for order showed in everything you did; your garden was as beautiful as your thoughtfulness and kindness. You have left a void which can never be filled.

To my Young Pioneer comrades at Hohoe, your encouragement helped me to continue performing onstage by reciting Osagyefo Dr. Kwame Nkrumah's speeches.

I would say those were my foundational moments which helped me to develop as a poet, a speaker and a storyteller.

Since my school days, I have always written the odd poem or two for friends on special occasions.

Mr. Higham, pastor of Heath Evangelical Church in Cardiff, gave me my first taste of seeing my work in print when a testimony I gave was printed in the church magazine.

To the memory of Mrs. Dorothy Jones; our afternoons together were filled with reading psalms, hymns and spiritual songs. You made such a fuss over my poem *A Deep Breath and a Tight Grip* that I finally got it published in my book *200 Years*.

My thanks go to pastor Tom Stables who encouraged me to add my poems and articles to the church newsletter. To the congregation at The Apostolic Church in Bridgend, your feedback and encouragement has brought me this far. You never belittled my small beginnings.

To my husband who patiently listened to and read my poems before anyone else, I am grateful for your kindness and allowing me to write sometimes until the early hours of the morning. Thank you also for the computer, laptop and tablet, given so I could write wherever and whenever I was inspired. Thank you for the confidence you continue to show in me.

To my children Mercy, Joel, Samuel Enoch and Esther Ann Adjepong, your interest in my work was such a tonic. Thank you all.

To the National Library of Poetry and the International Society of Poets; without the International Poet of Merit award, I would not have had the confidence to publish my books. Before my award I did not think my poems were good enough, but I wrote anyway. Some were published in my church newsletters and I wrote poems for friends on various occasions. After my award I sent 189 poems to my editor, Mr. Francis Beswick. He was very gracious and encouraged me to continue writing. He guided me through the process of grouping my work together for publication. I owe him a debt of gratitude for his assistance with my books.

The first edition of this book was published by Feather Books. My thanks go to Reverend John Waddington-Feather for making the publishing process less daunting, and for giving me the joy of seeing my first book in print. Thank you also for publishing some of my poems in "The Poetry Church".

# FOREWORD

When I received the International Poet of Merit award in 1999, many of my friends asked how I came to write poetry. I was also asked where I got my inspiration from. In the excitement of those moments, my immediate thoughts centred on the poems in old hymns and passages from the Bible.

Sixteen years ago I self-published three books of poetry, meditation and prayers;

*Olenso* - Poems and Memories of an African Village Girl

*Voice of Comfort* - Meditation and Prayers of an African Village Girl

*Solid Gold* - Meditation and Prayers of an African Village Girl

I have also published "*200 Years - Remember, Reflect and Respect*", another collection of my poems which I self-published in 2007 to mark the Bicentenary of the Act of the Abolition of the Trans-Atlantic Slave Trade, passed in March 1807. I could not call it a celebration as for me it was more of a discovery. It was the first time I had read in such detail books and online accounts of the slave trade. Naturally, I was shocked at the unspeakable cruelty my enslaved ancestors suffered.

The narrative of Fredrick Douglas compelled me to dedicate my book *200 Years* to his mother, Harriet Bailey, and to all who fought for the abolition of the slave trade.

The emotional pain evoked by our history has made it difficult for some people to broach the subject, but I felt that sharing in the pain of our history connected me in some way to the courage and endurance of those who suffered at the hands of their fellow men.

I have had time to reflect on the journey that brought me to writing poetry. Looking back, I received my first poetry award in 1958, just before my ninth birthday, when I was asked to recite a poem before the whole school in the presence of a visiting Education Officer.

The poem "I Vow to Thee My Country" rolled off my tongue with such expression (even though I did not understand what it meant) that the visiting Education Officer, the late Mr. A. C. Aforo, put his hand in his pocket and gave me a penny as a prize. I gave that penny to my mother, who was very proud of my achievement. That incident was to endear me to the Aforo family.

It was not a surprise that at Independence Day celebrations I was chosen to recite extracts from the speeches of Osagyefo Dr. Kwame Nkrumah, Ghana's first Prime Minister and first President. Before the gathering of chiefs, elders and dignitaries from the Buem Krachi area, I stood on the stage and recited;

> *"To negotiate with forces that are hostile on numbers of principle, is to sacrifice principle itself. Principle is indivisible; it is either wholly kept or wholly sacrificed. The slightest concession on matters of principle means the abandonment of principle."*

The applause from the crowd and praise from my teachers made me feel grateful that I was able to represent my school and family this way.

My mother, who never had the opportunity for formal education, was fascinated by the English language. She wished she could read and write, and made it her life's ambition to educate her children. She would proudly repeat some English words after us; which brought a lot of laughter into our home. We nicknamed her the "Old Lady", which she proudly accepted as her "English" name. Old age is something to be proud of in Ghana.

The African tradition of memorizing events, genealogy and customs was part of my mother's upbringing. She could decipher messages conveyed through the drum beat which was the means of communicating important events to surrounding villages before we had telephones.

For me poetry was everywhere; in music, dance, proverbs and idioms which the elders used to teach children. A wise child was expected to be a good listener who would be able to remember, connect and understand both verbal and non-verbal communication.

The customs and traditional ways of communicating were not always verbal.

When a younger person picked up a stone, walked up to an older person, usually a relative, and simply put the stone down and walked away, this was understood to be a confirmation of something the older person may have previously said to the younger person.

Most of the time, it would have been a warning from the older person which may not have been heeded by the younger person through lack of understanding. By this gesture the younger person confirmed the truth she or he discovered, and communicated the appreciation of the wisdom in that warning. It was a way of saying, "You were right!"

That simple action spoke volumes; the details of which was kept between the two people; who chose either to keep it between themselves or make it public. An observer would perceive the great importance of the act, but would have no right to pry.

The expression, "Mum or Dad this is your stone", dates back centuries in my tribe. Hand gestures, facial expressions and sometimes just silence communicated what words could not express.

This way of communicating may not be understood or even appreciated by people from different cultures. In my tribe people do not say everything that comes into their minds. When a person refuses to answer a question, it can mean that they simply do not wish to be drawn into whatever is being asked, or that the emotion associated with the subject is too raw and painful.

If the person does not know the answer they will answer plainly that they do not know.

So silence is not a sign of ignorance or being rude; it means something poignant which a wise person will acknowledge. They will then walk away or change the topic.

Poetry for me became a blend of verbal and non-verbal communication woven into the cultural fabric of my life.

I appreciate this custom even more when I read Ecclesiastes 3:7.*A time to tear apart and a time to sew together; a time to be silent and a time to speak.*

My love of poetry made me a favourite of some teachers, especially those who loved poetry themselves.

The list below contains some of the poems I loved to recite; which I also believe formed the foundation of the poet I am today;

"*The Seven Stages of Man*" and "*Under the Greenwood Tree*" by William Shakespeare

"*What Have We Done Today*" by Nixon Waterman

"*The Rime of the Ancient Mariner*" by Samuel Taylor Coleridge

"*The old order changeth, yielding place to new*" (from "*The Passing of Arthur*") by Lord Alfred Tennyson

"*My Sweetheart A Sailor He Sails On The Sea*", Author not known

"*How beautiful is the rain after the dust and heat*" (from "*The Rain in Summer*") by Henry Wadsworth Longfellow

"*Make friends as you go while the summer's aglow*", Author not known

"*The Aspiration of Youth*" ("*Higher, higher will we climb up the mount of knowledge*")

The poem which launched me into fame in my final year at school was Robert Southey's "*Bishop Hatto*".

Mrs. Senoo, headmistress of Gbi central RC Girls School in Hohoe, Ghana, loved poetry. It was she who introduced us to "*Bishop Hatto*". Memorizing all nineteen verses and reciting them put me on centre stage every Friday before the whole school. The rhyme and the emotions in the poem had a sad but expected end, as justice was done to the wicked bishop.

"*For they were sent to do judgment on him*"

To our young minds God's justice came to all who were wicked, even if they had a priestly office.

The poem "*Bishop Hatto*" became such a part of me that I would recite it to my growing children. I recited it recently at one of my storytelling sessions in a secondary school near my home in Shropshire, England. One student came to me later and expressed his desire to read and recite poetry.

Thank you, Robert Southey.

# INTRODUCTION

*Olenso*, the title of my first collection of poems, was dedicated to my maternal grandfather. I do not have any memory of him, but he left a great legacy of being a forthright, no-nonsense man who took good care of his family and community.

There was joy and light every time my mother spoke of her father and the respect attached to his name still resounds in my village. He now has many descendants. The traditions of the elders which reflected in the names given to their children have been the golden thread which has preserved our identity as a people and shaped our conduct towards each other and the people we come into contact with.

The meaning of a name becomes what the child and the community aspires to.

Olenso: "Life is not an arena for the show of strength." Your strength is not an excuse to pick a fight, but it surely would be an excuse to bring peace between warring factions. Physical, emotional, social and psychological strength commands respect in every community.

Your strength is the wisdom you bring; it is the peace you pursue, it is the confidence you give to the weak and your challenge to the bully, the unreasonable and foolish who bring conflict to divide communities.

These words are spoken over the child as their name is pronounced at a naming ceremony. The meaning of a child's name becomes a song and a poem a mother repeats to her child. As the child grows they learn to respond and answer to the name accordingly.

My daughter's first name is Mercy. Her name was chosen from Psalm 103:17-18:

*"As for man his days are like grass and as a flower of the field for he soon passes away; but the MERCY of the Lord is from everlasting to everlasting to them that fear him and his covenant and to them that remember his commandments to keep them."*

Every time I call my daughter's name, I also call on the mercy of the Lord into every situation; not only over her life but over my whole family. Thus I have treasured and carried on a great African tradition into my Christian life.

My world view has been shaped by my culture, education, faith and the many people I have been privileged to know, work with and those I have worshiped God with in my Christian journey.

Being a Christian has helped me to sift through the traditions of my tribe and glean from them the wisdom of generations which I believe God in His great mercy has endowed to every culture.

I believe that people of every language and culture have a deep longing for what is right and good. Cultures and traditions have evolved as people sought to resolve conflict and bring harmony to their communities. Many times these good intentions have been hijacked by cruel and evil men and women whose desire to dominate their societies has corrupted traditions with rituals and customs which hold people in bondage.

In many African cultures the mixture of good and not-so-good traditions has been a source of confusion to many Christians, so that some have thrown out the baby with the bathwater, whilst others have considered the bathwater as important if not more so than the baby.

Traditions either do not change at all, or if they do, change so slowly that centuries pass and we seem to be carrying the burdens our ancestors left. The thing that surprises me most is when some "Christians" seem to put their traditions above the word of God.

 The belief of some people that Christianity is the culture of "white people" makes it difficult for them to differentiate between God's word and culture. There may be some things even in church traditions which have very little to do with the gospel of Christ.

Recently, in 2010, when a Christian group had wanted to put the story of our Lord's death and resurrection on Easter eggs, some supermarkets in England questioned "what Jesus had to do with Easter".

When traditions are not explained, they lose their meaning. I would not like to be proud of my culture and traditions without fully understanding their meaning and significance. In my tribe it is *taboo* to question some elements of our traditions.

It is considered disrespectful to question the wisdom of the ancestors who died centuries ago. Unfortunately there is no way to find out if some of the excesses in rituals were part of their original plan.

The shortcoming of the oral traditions, and I daresay that of most traditions, are that without examining and questioning them, they go stale and lose their relevance.

In my collection of poems, I have tried to use threads of the good I find in my culture, which is in harmony with what is revealed in God's word, to create the pulse of a heartbeat which unites us as people on the same planet. If I may borrow from the Death of King Arthur:

*The old order changeth, yielding place to new, And*
*God fulfils Himself in many ways*
*Lest one good custom should corrupt the world.*
*Comfort thyself: what comfort is in me?*
*I have lived my life, and that which I have done*
*May He within himself make pure!"*
                    By Lord Alfred Tennyson.

Though the old order continues to change, it is by gleaning from the old values that makes sense of the new order.

Olenso, my grandfather's name, means a lot in our world today. Life is not an arena for the show of strength. May those who think they can use their strength to oppress the weak take note.

# Chapter 1
# The Traditional Stool

# OLENSO

Olenso, the brave man and the hunter in an African
village
Olenso, my maternal grandfather
though I never knew him his name has been like a light
that guides
Olenso, it is not about strength
*It is not a strong man who always picks a fight*
*for life is not an arena for the show of strength*
So he lived and died but left his name for us to
remember
*There is more strength in the man who refuses to fight*
*just to show how strong he is*
*There is more strength in peace than in war.*
*yet there is a time when men must fight*
*for the good of all*
*Unity is safety*
*The people who fight among themselves*
*will have no strength to turn back an invading army*
Joining the wrong crowd for a meaningless fight
is wasting strength that tills the land
The energy used to break somebody's jaw
could be used to make a row of yam mounts
There is strength in Africa
that feeds and clothes families
A strong man keeps and protects his family
His children are not ashamed of him

There are people who believe in being seen
others are known
Nana Kwaku Olenso
how true these sayings are even today
I dedicate this book to all your descendants
that we may all come to know another strong man
who became weak on the cross to save mankind
His last prayer was for unity for all who follow Him
I wish you knew Him too

# THE TRADITIONAL STOOL

The traditional stool has a great significance. It is a symbol of stability, humility, strength and wisdom. The stool invites you to sit and listen. All important matters are discussed sitting down. "We will sit and talk" means we need to give time and thought to the topic or the issue. The elders sit down before sending for the parties in dispute.

It is considered disrespectful to stand and talk or argue about things. The sitting position is believed to help a person calm down and collect thoughts together.

Let's sit and talk. Your opinion may differ but we can show respect to each other when we sit and talk.

In my tribe, a father would give a woven cloth and new traditional stool to his daughter as wedding presents. The new stool points the bride to a new beginning. She carries the new stool to her marital home when she sits on that stool; she is proclaiming that she is in her own home.

She is instructed to sit and talk through every issue with her husband. The stool also tells her to stay in the marriage. She will sit on the stool to do many household chores and teach her children the wisdom of the ancestors. The woven cloth is symbol of strength, durability and beauty. She would wear that cloth on special occasions to show that she has come from a good home.

# AUNTIE KOTIAH
## (A childhood memory)

We were nearly there. We could see the houses in the distance, and the occasional sounds of village life could be heard. We had journeyed for miles on foot. It was the rainy season and the dusty road had turned muddy in places. We tried without success to avoid the mud. Dust can be shaken off but mud is something else, especially when it dries up and cakes on your sandals and toes as you walk along.

There was a sigh of relief when the houses appeared on the horizon. Nearly there now.

It was always good to see old auntie Kotiah and all our other relatives of the extra-extended family. Everyone was called either auntie or uncle. Great cousins were simply called brothers and sisters.

Old auntie was mother's eldest sister. Since my grandmother died before I was born she became the grandma I never had. She was love itself, full of excitement and joy though she was crippled in her lower limbs.

She moved about by walking on her knees, dragging her legs and feet along and supporting her hands on a wooden stool. She had had an accident and hurt her back, which crippled her. Thankfully her children were grown up when this happened. She continued to do everything as before, except go to the farm. She became the mender of clothes. Most of our relatives brought clothes for her to mend for them. They kept her busy so she would feel useful when they were at their farms.

She always kept very busy, was pleasant and well loved. I can never remember her feeling sorry for herself or anybody else feeling sorry for her. Rather she received love and respect from everybody.

It was as if her handicap meant nothing. We loved her so much and she loved us.

The joy of seeing her again, her broad smiling face, grey hair, and her musical voice, was what made our periodic journeys to her worthwhile.

We all knew mother was a great cook (though she made no noise about it). Some lorry drivers who have had meals at our home brought their wives and left them with mother; requesting that she teach them to cook soups and stews of all kinds. She should have written a cookery book.

Yet it was auntie Kotiah's soups that I looked forward to every time we visited Okraye where she lived.

Kyemekopo was a special place because that was where Mum and Dad lived until a crisis in the family forced them to move. I guess that was why I could not warm up to it as I did to Okraye.

As we journeyed near the village we came into a swamp. The heavy rains had made a nearby stream burst its banks. The soil was a mixture of mud and clay, which made the ground slippery. Water came up to my knees, but only to the ankles of my big sisters. We all carried things to sell; gifts of soap, pomade, talc, sweets and other goodies which were not available at Okraye.

Mother was the much travelled one. She was a farmer, a trader and ran a cooked food bar. She almost always gave away more things than she sold. It seemed to be a tradition, this giving away of everything that can be given.

The nature of the goods we were carrying on our heads dictated that we could not allow ourselves to fall in the swamp. To avoid the slippery ground (which used to be the road) we had to walk on the sides where grass and shrubs provided grips to prevent us from falling.

The journey came to a standstill as one of my big sisters walked slowly ahead to assess how deep the swamp would be, or how slippery, or if there were any stumps of old trees which may have sharp edges.

At the end my sisters divvied up my load of goodies and added them to their own, just so that if I slipped and fell, they would not have to search for the bars of Lux and Resona soaps in the muddy waters. It was a relief not to be carrying anything. It was easy to look around and notice all the butterflies and the tsetse flies as well!

"Just don't let them sting you," said big sister, "they cause diseases. Now that you are not carrying anything use this piece of cloth to swat them from your body - and also from us."

So we journeyed very slowly until we were safely out of the swamp. As we entered the village, the message rang out, "They are here!" Children ran to auntie Kotiah with the message. She lived at the other end of the village. Our other relatives ran to meet us, and took our loads from us. That was the tradition. If they had known we were coming they would have met us at the swamp (I am sure Mum would not have asked us to travel if she had known about the swamp). After all that excitement, I ran into auntie Kotiah's arms and sat on the floor in her room.

Her house always had a special touch, her room was always cool. Her floor was made of the traditional red gravel mixed with the binding agent they produce from the bark of a special tree. The bark of the tree was dried and then soaked in water until it released the freshness of wood perfume and acted as a binding agent, which binds gravel and makes it look like concrete.

Women had specially made flattened pieces of wood with which they flattened this wonderful floor covering into place. This was done to music as it helped the work along. Singing while you worked was the norm.

The perfume of the bark of the tree remained in the house, adding freshness to the rooms.

It is a shame that floors are no longer made this way. I guess it is due to the sheer hard work involved, and also because cement and marble floors are more in fashion nowadays - not forgetting that most people who can afford carpets and rugs use them instead.

It was always good to be home with auntie Kotiah who could not stop hugging us and remarking how we had all grown since she last saw us.

After we had a drink of water from *calabashes*, other relatives came around to give us the traditional welcome. We had to tell them all about our journey, also extending to them greetings from Mum and relatives in our village. Auntie Kotiah was most concerned when we told her of the swamp. "Oh, I am glad nobody fell in those muddy waters. The river Oti has also burst its banks, I am told, and the hills are all very slippery indeed," she remarked. Meanwhile one of our cousins had started cooking yams. It was evening and the golden sun was gently sliding behind the hills and throwing long shadows of trees around.

The farmers were returning from their farms and the music of pestle and mortar pounding could be heard from the houses of those having *fufu*[1] for supper. We were having *fufu* as well. It was always a treat. Auntie Kotiah made the soup. Almost all the girls my age came

---

[1] *Fufu is boiled yam or cassava and green plantain pounded to soft dough. It is eaten with a choice of palm, peanut butter or light soup made with fish, chicken or meat and with vegetables. (Sorry, no recipes!)*

around after supper and we played games of *ampeh*[2] and *Amaye! Amaye!*[3]

There were so many new songs to learn. Funny stories, news about engagements, marriages and babies being born were shared. My friends filled me in with everything they thought I should know. A new bride (*okofor*) is called so for a whole year, and she wore special beads which identified her as such.

The following day we went to greet everybody in the village, staying longer with those who had been bereaved or ill or recently engaged. Tradition demanded that.

All our relatives would bring food to auntie Kotiah's house as a sign of welcome to us. There was always so much food, but I preferred auntie Kotiah's. How I treasure the memories of her.

---

[2] *Ampeh is a game played by young girls, taking the lead role in turns, the leader jumps and sticks one foot out. The players must anticipate which foot and do the same. If the leader is caught out her place is taken over and she joins the ranks. This is done to singing and clapping.*

[3] *Amaye! Amaye! is also for young girls. A group of six to eight girls stand in a semi-circle, taking it in turns, each girl in response to songs would throw herself backwards to be caught by the group. There are no winners in this game. It is played for fun and trusting friends not to allow you to fall.*

# ACCEPTING KINDNESS

Kindness sees a need and offers some relief. Those who have been in real need are grateful even for a short relief.

The expectation of kindness and giving has been so woven into the Ghanaian and the African culture that sometimes it is taken for granted that those who appear to have something are obliged to give to whoever they meet. Giving and receiving is part of our culture, so it is not embarrassing to tell your neighbour or relative that you have a need.

I would like to add that if this had not been part of our culture, so many people would have become homeless. Many families sacrifice to help each other by giving their time to look after sick relatives' children and orphans.

They don't expect to be paid for this service because not only is it part of the culture, but most of the time those in need have no way of paying for the services rendered. They would reciprocate at some point in their lives.

Growing up in a village means you were taught whose house you may consider as your own among your many relatives or whose clothes you may borrow for an occasion.

As in other cultures there are people who may show kindness but will never keep quiet about it. Prudence discerns who to take from or who to give to.

Takers in every society expect the earth itself to be given to them forgetting that God in His kindness has already given the earth to us all for in our short life span.

One of the many things my mother taught me which I

deeply cherish is; No one owes me anything so I should appreciate kindness no matter how insignificant it may seem. Accepting kindness is also accepting the person who gives it. Kindness should have no strings attached. There is joy in giving to those in need because nobody knows when they too may be in need.

She taught me that the biggest gift I would receive is when someone thinks about me. They may not be in a position to offer me anything but the fact that a person says; "I have been thinking about you" is a sentiment to be treasured.

# THE OVERGROWN PATH

The overgrown path speaks for itself
It has not been used for quite some time
yet it may have be a path you have used before

Neglect is something even a humble path
does not wish to experience
whether it is a hobby, a friendship or a daily chore
neglect soon starts to show

What is beginning to look like an overgrown path
in your life?
What has caused the neglect
which is becoming evident to those around you?

Perseverance and determination
turn paths into well-travelled roads

The Ghanaian Adinkra symbol of Sankofa
encourages us to retrace our steps
to retrieve something of value
we have lost or neglected
Start that journey again today
Though the path be overgrown
it will soon yield to the footfall of a familiar friend
Send that text message
write that letter
complete that project
It still awaits your touch.
There is something of value on every overgrown path

# LIFE WAS SO SIMPLE THEN

I grew up in a village where people did not have much, but it seemed as if there was really nothing to worry about.

Everything was hard work, but nobody complained because that was how we lived. If you did not go to the farm or if you did not roam the jungle to fetch firewood, you had no food to eat, unless you were one of the very rich people who bought firewood and farm produce; but even they soon found that their money did not stretch far enough.

That was simply how it was; and people were happy. When someone died the whole village came together to mourn and comfort the bereaved. Yes, like all human societies, there were quarrels, even fights, some of which were entertaining, especially if the fights were between rival wives.

Disputes were however quickly settled, as the elders had the responsibility to maintain a peaceful atmosphere in the village. The medicine men and the fetish priests believed that conflict of any sort between people resulted in disease or natural disasters, and most people did not want to be accused or held responsible for thunder storms, floods, and drought or disease epidemics.

Even a child contracting malaria, dysentery or measles would be because of some dispute or grudge held between family members. Difficult childbirth, maternal and infant mortality were all blamed on some unresolved issue which had displeased the gods and the ancestors.

Children were taught never to repeat words which were taboo. Women would click their fingers behind both ears to avert some disaster which happened somewhere else, saying, "May God send it far from our borders".
People knew what was expected of them; the respect for tradition and the elders of society brought harmony to the community.
Life is simple when you know what is expected of you and when you know you belong to a community. It takes unexpected change to appreciate that life was so simple then.

# WHEN IT BOILS

A kettle switches off when it comes to boil or boils dry. An old Ghanaian proverb says, "when it boils, it also cools down."

Nothing boils forever so we are told not to let the sun go down on our anger. Let it cool off so you can have a good night's sleep. How kind to yourself that would be. A good night's sleep is important for your energy and creativity. When anger robs you of sleep, you wake up tired, frustrated and even angrier.

The world has a record of leaders who inspired their followers to commit genocide against other people. These leaders rose and fell even if they believed they might rule forever. History has a record of men and women who in their time thought they were appointed to purge the world of people who did not fit into their definition of a perfect race. They all came to an end but left the world in shock at what human cruelty can do.

Today, because of what we know, we look at leaders differently. We know that in our tribes and nations we do not live in isolation. The people we think are our enemies may yet become our friends. Have there not been enough mass graves to humble us? From every continent the history of slavery, forced labour, greed and exploitation of children bears witness to how the rich take advantage of the poor.

Some men and women think their fellow human being was put on earth for their comfort. But there is time appointed for all to die and give account of how we lived.

When it boils, it also cools down. When you hear leaders who vow to wipe out other nations, remember it has happened before but people live on. Only God retains the power to wipe us all out if He chooses to. Let history's lessons humble us in the estimation of ourselves and other people so we can live and let others live. For there is an account to give to Him who made us from dust.

# CULTURES

A question, only a question
Answers are hard to find
but sometimes questions answer questions
Cultures, what are cultures?
So varied, so complicated yet so simple

What are cultures?
Are cultures what defined people?
Tribes? Families?
Are cultures the cords woven by men and women of old
to bind their people together
giving them a sense of belonging and safety?
Cultures, what are cultures?
Do cultures define difference in the way we think
and respond to situations?
Are we all like children carefully and lovingly fed
at the table of our cultures?

Cultures like foods we have grown to love and enjoy?
Do they become our first choice when we find a table
spread with cuisines unfamiliar to us?
Can we trust that some other people's cultures
were woven with similar cords?
Cords of love, safety, respect, loyalty?
Can we see beauty in the ways of others?
Though we may not fully understand their ways
and why they do the things they do?

Why do all cultures mourn their dead?
Why do all cultures rejoice

at the news of a new baby born?
Why do people of all cultures fall in love?
Why do people of all cultures suffer from broken hearts?

Are the things we feel universally
woven in our cultures
or were our cultures woven in response
to what nature makes us feel?
We hear of new worlds, first worlds and third worlds
cultures which have survived since creation cannot
suddenly have sprung up in first place
or drop down to third
If cultures were all woven with similar materials
of love, safety, respect and loyalty
why is it then difficult to respect each other's cultures?

Why is it as if we are threatened
when other cultures camp on our door step?
Cultures in centuries past
denied the rights of other people
the right to live freely in their own land
People of old expanded their cultures
by introducing other cultures
by invading other cultures
yet see how those cultures have remained intact.
Is it after all about belonging, loving,
respecting and being loyal?

Cultures, what are cultures?
A question's only a question
Answers are hard to find
but sometimes questions answer questions

# CULTURAL HERITAGE

How was anybody to know, even anticipate
the changes that would take place
at the time when we were accounted
as less than nothing?

The ridicule of the woman
who sent her children to school
What were her dreams, hopes, aspirations?
Who was to know how it would end?
Watching those who had made it
those who were the somebodies of society
who was to know that a time would come
when the changes would turn everything around?

There is hope for all who dare to hope
for those who learn to put their trust in God
Moments change and people change
Situations alter but those who hope in God
will find that He never changes
Always the same, ever faithful to his wayward children

I come home after a long time away
and find that so much has changed
I like to think that I have not changed
except in age and in size
but I find that my values have changed
my sense of belonging taken a few knocks

I still belong
This is my home
These are my people
but this is no longer a culture I wish to ascribe to
a culture that humiliates its people
A culture unkind to the widow
and uncaring towards the orphan
A culture that pushes its people into sin

Sadly the things that gave a sense of community
those values which were worth keeping
have been abandoned
The caring nurturing in the village has disappeared
and no one mourns
The land suffers from neglect
The people don't care anymore about family values
yet they hold on to the outdated customs
which push people into degradation
if not insanity

# ANOTHER KIND OF POVERTY

There is another kind of poverty, he said
Not having someone to share life with
is a kind of poverty
though a person could have everything
That kind of poverty
causes the same emotional pain
as not being able to meet financial needs
Poverty causes pain
Physical, emotional and spiritual pain

Hunger causes physical pain
Lack of what we need causes emotional pain
and the feeling of worthlessness causes spiritual pain
There is an innate desire to do good
to share and enjoy life
with another person or a circle of friends
When this is not achieved
the feeling of failure destroys
a person's sense of worth

Sleeping on the cold damp floor in the subway
is a man who may have known and shared love
may have held a job
and had a circle of friends
He is still an important member
of a community, a family, a nation
but here he lies on the cold damp floor
on which the cardboard box has no effect
He relies on the human family
to throw a few coins by his side
so he could buy a hot drink
The people walk past
some give
others do not see him as part of their problem
They walk on into their busy world
Poverty is the lack of what you need
food, clothes, warmth, friendship, love, laughter
and someone to care for
Man or woman is not meant to live life alone

# WHAT A PRICE FOR A DREAM

The dream of a lifetime
The illusion
to live in a developed country
to find a job and save a lot of money
then to come back home and settle down
Who said the streets were paved with gold?
and where is the job
which will make me save some money?

Was it a dream?
Was it a nightmare?
How do I make ends meet
and send money to the folks back home?
I sent some photos of me in nice clothes
Bless him, they said, he looks well suited
I wonder how many wish they were me
living here
unable to find a lasting job
And I bet some may even envy me because I live abroad

I struggled for forty years
My kids have grown and left home
It is hard to grow old here
my bones can't stand the winter anymore
Home in the sunshine where I'll pay no winter bills
This too has become a dream
like the dream that brought me here
I dream of the quiet village life
of old friends and relatives

Surely they will welcome me back with open arms
We will talk again about the good old days
It will be nice to touch and feel the earth again
when I grow my own food
I do not have a lot of savings but I have my pension
That will go a long way back home
where I'll have no bills to pay

The dream burns in my heart
and I start to put together the things I need
The time draws near and now
I remember the hard times no more
the prejudice I suffered
and how I could never really make this place my home
I look forward
oh how I look forward
to going back home
At last
heavens be blessed
I am home!

What has happened?
Things have changed.
Why have they all changed so much?
They treat me like a total stranger
an outsider
as though I committed a crime for going to live abroad
No, I have changed
Goodness, did I really change so much?
I laugh at things nobody considers funny
Customs I have forgotten
They feel I am mocking them

They tell me to go back to where I came from
That is what I have heard for the past forty years
Go back where you came from
This country does not belong to you
For forty years
I lived as a stranger in another man's land

I come home, and I am a stranger to my own people
They look at me, they watch my ways
What have I done wrong?
Where did I go wrong?

What a price to pay for a dream
I have one last dream
That one day soon when death shall knock on my door
I will be accepted
among those who have gone on before
I wonder
will they too say to me
go back to where you came from?

# WISDOM IN A JAR
*(My early years in Britain)*

The old shopkeeper smiled as he came to my help.
"What are you looking for?" he asked.
I had been browsing for over an hour in this shop that sold almost everything. I was not sure if I should tell him or what he would say if I did.
He looked searchingly in my eyes expecting an answer
"Wisdom", I answered, "A jar of wisdom to be precise."
He looked puzzled and asked,
"What kind of thing is it? Is it jam? Powder? Seeds? Nuts? Oil?"
"No. Wisdom. You know, something to make me wise."
I said.
"And it comes in a jar?" he asked with a mixture of amusement and intrigue.
His wife, who had been watching me like a hawk the minute I entered the shop, came over to us and asked,
"What does the young woman want?"
"Wisdom", he said, looking at his wife as if to ask for help.
She was a woman who had answers to every question under the sun. "Health food shop down the road!" she said, pointing me to the door with a tone of voice army commanders would envy.
The old man looked at his wife, then at me, and said,
"I never knew wisdom came in jars, whatever next."
"Oh darling, these days they can buy everything, even new bodies" said his wife eager to close the chapter.
"Except brains and bones," I added, wishing she would see the funny side and smile.

27

But she was a stern woman, and as I walked through the door I noticed the dear old man still puzzled, looking at his wife as if they have just had some visitor from outer space. I wonder how long they would be talking about this, and if someone would really go to a health food shop and ask for wisdom in a jar.

Talking to people and learning from them had become a pastime for me. Being in a foreign land, with different tastes and values, I had to find a way of getting to know people.

Older people I found had time to talk and share, they also had a sense of humour that struck a chord with me. Asking for wisdom in a jar from shopkeepers always brought laughter, and opened the way to conversation, but I was to learn that different people needed a different approach.

One shopkeeper suggested I asked the dentist, as he thought it was something to rub on a wisdom tooth.

The accent of a foreigner has its own disadvantages, and some people have not got the patience for people "who can't speak English".

It is either "Sorry, we haven't got it," or, "Try the market."

Most of the time it was best to look hard, find what you were looking for, and take it to the till, or write it on a piece of paper if your hand writing is decipherable.

Looking for wisdom in a jar, what did I find? The old man I was sure would have delivered the goods if his wife had not interrupted. He had a look on his face which would have broken into laughter if we had continued our banter.

Was his wife always so abrupt with all their customers?
Or was it because I was a foreigner?
Surely she must have known I was just a waste of time,
asking for wisdom in a jar.

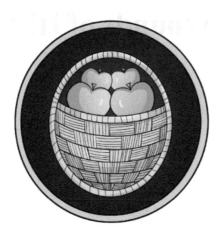

# Chapter 2
# The Wounds of History

# MY SISTER?

My sister, I cannot reach you
You have been gone for far too long
Our united lives were torn apart
Torn apart by man's inhumanity to man
But our bond still remains when we smile
I know you are my sister
and you know I am yours

What you speak I cannot understand
My language only strange noises to your ear
But when our eyes meet and we smile
we both know we are at home with each other
Your views and your tastes have changed
we stand many centuries apart
My home is so different to yours
my bare feet crack at the soles

You watch me with pity
as I work all day in the heat of the sun
When you see my suffering
when you hear my woes
something stirs deep in your soul
I see it in your eyes
I know you feel my pain
When you smile you share my joy
we communicate by soul
That is where I reach you
because your skin and my skin
will not express what we feel

# WE MEET AGAIN

We meet again
not that we have met before
unless my heart and soul deceive me
Your face and your smile
emanate a love that is so familiar
a love so warm, so true
yet you walk away
afraid that you will be hurt again
spiritual memory surfacing
forcing you to raise the barriers that deny love
walking away again
making me feel the searing pain of loss
of betrayal and of separation
You walk away as if our love never existed
You walk away
making my attempt to communicate feel like a nuisance
You know and I know
I hope you know that an unseen cord connects us
A cord history has not been able to break
but it has left its pull in each of us
though we have been separated for centuries
by man's inhumanity towards his fellow man

# A LONG TIME AGO

All you had was only half of what it should be
You made it whole
turning it around and reshaping it
It looked complete in your hands
You cherished it and held it close to your heart
until you come in contact with the broken half

You are surprised
It should have fitted perfectly with what you had
Now you can see what the complete should have looked
like

But you turned and reshaped it
smoothing those edges
to conceal the rough jagged end left there
to fit the broken half when they are reunited

Two halves standing side by side
unable to be rejoined
The smooth and the rough
Once upon a time the two halves were a complete whole

Do not think that all you have is all there is
Look again
and be willing to accept
that once upon a time
I was the other part of you
and you were the other part of me

# WE DID NOT TRAVEL BY THE CONCORDE

We did not travel by the Concorde
We would have got there in hours
We did not travel by a jumbo jet
We would have had very good company
We did not travel by train.
We would have made many stops on the way,

We did travel by sea
sometime on our journey
The entertainment eased the boredom
but we were the entertainment

We did not travel by bus or car or motorcycle
so we did not travel so-many-miles-per-hour
Our journey was on foot

Foot chained to foot
arm to arm
neck to neck

We travelled step by step
inch by inch
The step behind determined by the step in front
For our captors, that must have been an entertainment

But what patience they must have had.
walking alongside
step by step
inch by inch
watching
so we did not break free from the chains
Yet the closeness to each other
linked together by chain
was the refreshment we had on the way
We were alone but not alone
We were together.
Step by step
inch by inch
the chains provided the music

We did not travel by Concorde
Nor did we travel by train
We travelled on foot first
before we were thrown into boats
to destinations known only by our captors
Silently we stood as bids were made for us
by those rich enough
to own their fellow human beings

Made of a different colour
and speaking a different language
The cargo was human

We have travelled a long way
We have come very far
Societies have formed
to prevent cruelty to child and mother
battered sore
to protect the unborn and their unsure mothers

Now we travel by Concorde, the jumbo jet and the train
Now we travel by bus, by car and motorcycles
and ferries and ships
We meet each other and it seems we still hear a noise
made by the chains that bound our ancestors

We look at each other and smile.
We sing and clap
releasing from deep inside all we have not had the
courage to say
deeply buried from long ago
Goosebumps still rise
for it is a song and a cry from long ago
when our music was provided by chains

We have societies to protect birds and elephants,
the animals in the wild, the fish in the sea
Dogs and cats now have protection
from humans cruel enough to hurt them
They are protected from humans who not so long ago
Did worse to their fellow humans

# WE LOOK FOR THE BONES

We look for the bones
scattered abroad a long time ago
We look for our brothers and sisters
aunties and uncles
We look for them
Bones so mixed up, scattered and thrown abroad
they are not easy to find

"Why would you look for the bones
of those you sold into slavery?
Why would you care where they laid?"
You have pain in your heart
I have pain in mine
No mother ever sold her child in those bygone days
No brothers or sisters ever consented
to be deprived of the ones they loved

In your grief you forget the grief of the mothers
who went to their graves mourning lost children
It may have happened long ago
but something of their pain still lives through us
the same way the pain of being sold still lives
in your heart
We have all been hurt
and robbed of each other

You choose to forget
the pain and anguish of your brothers and sisters
and the relatives of those who were taken away

Those they never heard from and never saw again
That is why we look for the bones
We search the faces of those we meet
We see resemblance in faces

In stature, in voice, even in manners
we feel a strong bond of family ties
of belonging to those who may think of us
as total strangers
sometimes even enemies
We look at each other
sometimes we smile
Other times the wall of silence remains
and we wonder what the other is thinking
or feeling

That seems to be all we can do now
since we cannot find the bones
We have not been able to talk about the things
which cause us deep pain
sometimes embarrassment
We all know this pain will not go away
It remains like a hole in our hearts
When we meet with the stark resemblance
of our relatives
their smiles and their manner of speech
even their voices
send a chill down the spine

But what can we do?
You know your pain
I know mine
Yet there is that "something"
like a spiritual bond
makes me want to run and embrace you
like a mother finding a lost child
When the child walks away
oblivious to the mother's pain
there are no words to describe
the devastation she feels.

You suffered from the slave trade?
I suffered more
but when are we going to talk about it?
We all suffered from the void that cannot be filled
The past was cruel
the past was evil
but we live on
You in me, I in you
We are one.
We may not find the bones
but we can find each other.
Brothers and sisters
aunties and uncles
separated for centuries
but still drawn together by some unseen hand
when we are willing to acknowledge the pain
we all feel

# LET US NOT FORGET

The men and women of conviction
who fought to make the world a better place
They saw how evil and unacceptable
the way of life was in their time
In their bellies a fire burned a fire of truth
of fair play
of love
and the good of humanity
They risked their lives
and sacrificed their comforts
for those being trodden under foot
Let us not forget them

Today we are free, so it seems to us
free to enjoy the fruits
of the labours of those who fought
They would be proud
to see how far we have come today
they would be proud
to see their dreams come true
In our freedom let us not forget
that evil still lives in our streets
that children are still dying
from starvation, disease, drugs and guns
that some of our human brothers and sisters
have nowhere to live or sleep
and no food to eat.

We pass by them in the streets
as though they were none of our business
These were some of the things
men and women of old fought for
these were some of the things
that kept them awake at night
They met with each other
they prayed together
they wept about injustice
Then they planned to rid this world
of evil and cruelty, shame and deprivation
They worked hard
some did not live to see the fruit of their labour
Their work is done, the fruits remain

What about us?
Are we only going to sit and talk
about the evil that stalks our streets
and do little about it?
It is sad how we are able to sleep at night
when only yesterday our children were shot dead
by children they used to play with
Somehow we feel so helpless
we call it the signs of the times
The men and women of years gone by could not sleep
They prayed, they did something.
They risked their lives,
sacrificed their comforts
and made sure the streets of their world were safe
Let us not forget them.
Let us be inspired, as we appreciate the work they did
Let us learn to be like them.

# THE WOUNDS OF HISTORY

The wounds of history still bleed
whether they are hundreds of years old or two decades
The wounds of history are nasty and deep
until they are uncovered and treated

The wounds of history stay in the dark because they are
shameful and disgusting
They upset us and create deep anger in us
The wounds of history have a way of affecting us today
covered up in layers of lies, denial and dust
they continue to putrefy and cause pain
the longer we avoid them or give excuses for them

The wounds of history will continue
to cause embarrassment and anger
Sadly even today in many towns and cities
new wounds are being inflicted
because the wounds of history keep being repeated

Man's inhumanity to man
Man's lack of courage to confront the wrongs of society
Man's indifference towards his fellow man
Man's foolishness in thinking he can do what he likes
to satisfy his selfish desires without consequence

Throughout history man has committed
shameful crimes with impunity
using excuses which called wrong right and evil good

Man has enslaved his fellow man
treated him with shameful cruelty
and made profit from it
Nations have exploited other nations
enslaved them with their rules and contracts
brought generations into bondage and poverty

Women and children have been raped repeatedly
while those appointed into office to protect them
turned a blind eye
For decades the victims lived lives
devoid of the sense of worth
but the wounds of history are being uncovered
Shameful horrid wounds
inflicted by the base and the respectable alike
using modern technology as tools
for their shameful acts

Could  the bleeding wounds of history
be the reason for continued bloodshed today?

# MILLENNIUM AFRICA

Back to the prison where he was kept
for twenty and six years
Mr. Nelson Mandela
Back to the memories of dark days
where hope flickered like a candle light
in the dark African night

There he lit a candle
the flame of love and hope
and handed it to his predecessor
then quietly gently passing it to the children
whose hope for tomorrow must burn
brighter than a candle light

Standing in a line that marked the borders
of the African continent
Their candles flickered in the African night
welcoming a new millennium with life and hope.
Theirs was not the excess of other nations.
No razzmatazz, no parties that cost
two-thousand pounds a head
in the prison where he was kept.

He knows too well, the fragile steps
his people must take.
After years of being trodden under foot
by those who are still learning
it is possible for all men to live together side by side
He lights the candle on his own behalf
and on behalf of all those who died in the fight.

His hope is that the past will be a history
that will not repeat itself for generations yet unborn
as they reach out
to a future of peace, tolerance and understanding
a future where domination of one culture over another
and one people over others
will be unnecessary.

Today he walks slowly
gently
the man on whom age is taking its toll
but whose smile radiates the ageless warmth
of those whose determination liberates the soul
and carry the flame of freedom from deep within
Africa, may you continue to give your very best
though for centuries your wealth exploited.

Of gold and diamonds, timber, tea and coffee
cocoa and spices
Your wildlife has been shipped and flown across
to many nations of the world caged
they live in zoos.
Your sons and daughters
sold as slaves
survived
Their descendants bless the world with talents
not thought possible by their captors
who denied that they were humans
Africa, heart and soul of freedom of all who live in you
A home of warmth, hospitality and drumbeat
you refuse no one
from the ant to the elephant
to all men who will live in peace.

HAPPY MILLENNIUM, AFRICA!

*(It was a pleasant surprise to receive a response from
Mr. Nelson Mandela for a copy of this poem.)*

# THE CRUELTY CONTINUES

Centuries have passed since the cruel trade ended, but in the hearts and souls of some men and women the dark, wicked spirit of cruelty has taken a deep root.

They hurt at the thought that all men are created equal. In their hearts and minds the cruelty seeks to turn back the clock.

Their speech and actions betray their innermost thoughts. With hatred in their souls they plan and scheme to trap innocent black men who may through lack of knowledge break the law by walking on the wrong side of the street.

Because to some who should be upholding the law skin colour alone makes people guilty until proven innocent, if the circumstances allow that innocence to be proven.

That is why I feel that the proportion of black men in prisons exceeds any other ethnic group.

Racism after all is the tail end of the wicked trade in human beings.

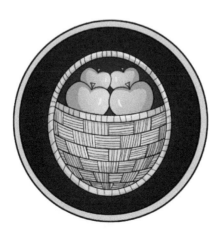

# Chapter 3
# The Darkness of War

# WHEN YOU PREPARED FOR WAR

When you prepared yourself to fight
who was the battle against?
When you called your men of war together
and assigned them positions
who did you think you were fighting?
The battle was arrayed
the supply of arms abundant
but who was it you fought?

Daily the volunteers came from far and near
You had more than you could ever need
When you prepared yourself for war
who did you think your enemy was?
How did you assess His strength?
How long were you prepared to stand against Him?
When you prepared yourself to fight against your unseen
enemy?

Why were your missiles so ineffective?
Why did you have to use so much ammunition
without hitting a single target?
When you prepared yourself to fight
who was it that you fought?
Did you know that His purpose was not to fight?
When you called your men of war together
when you assigned positions

did you see Him bleed?
bleed with love and pity for you?
When you prepared yourself for war
did you know that He had already fought
and won the battle for you?
that He stood not as an enemy but as a friend?
Did you know that in fighting Him who loves you
you fight against yourself?

Why are your men so exhausted?
so exhausted, yet they fight on
supposing that victory might yet be won
When you prepared yourself to fight
did you know that the enemy you fought against was
Love?
That is why He rose again from the dead

He is always the winner because His love never dies
When you fight and when I fight
we fight in vain against His love
for no weapon formed against Him will prosper
When we lay down our arms before Him we also
discover that no weapon formed against us will prosper
When we fight against each other
we fight against He who laid down His life for us.

*(Sometimes those things we fight against may be sent for
our blessing.)*

# DOING THEIR DUTY

They tossed and turned
unable to sleep they reached for the gin
The alcohol helped them to sleep
only to wake up to another day of doing their duty
They lied through their teeth
as they led the innocent victims
to the gas chambers
daily doing their duty

Where was guilt?
Where was shame?
Where was that "something inside"
that made them different from the animals of the wild?
They cushioned themselves with the thought
of doing their duty

The screams reached their ears
screams of women and children
of young and old
but they were just doing their duty

Naked bodies were laid pile upon pile
no names
no next of kin informed
by the men just doing their duty

They got home at night and reached for the gin
the potion that dulled the senses
of men doing their duty

In the morning they greeted each other
laughed and joked
like men doing their duty

What is your duty?
Is it a duty?
The screams must ring in their ears long into the future
the piles of human bodies remain
when the gin can no longer dull the senses
of men doing their duty

# IF THERE WERE NO WARS

The attraction may well be inbuilt
so in every generation young men and women
join the army
They see and experience things
that remain in their memories for a long time
They sense that wars must be fought
Their innocent lives are lost

The unmarked graves
not forgetting families torn apart and destroyed
Who won the war?
The silent in graves will never know.
Who won the war?
Those who live with injured memories may always ask
The graves of the fallen are tended and kept immaculate
Bodies of young men
some too young to have any one bear their names
except the gravestones

Yet we continue to fight wars
men and women continue to enlist
because the whole world has no code of conduct
Greed, bigotry, shameless barbarism
still inflict their wounds on us.

The pain of destruction
the unforgiving wounds of crimes
committed in centuries gone by
and the greed of power and control
are an endless recipe
for killing and maiming and destroying
not only each other
but the world we live in.

Tomorrow there may be
yet another reason to go to war
while we are still nursing those who lost their limbs
in a war that has hardly ended
The attraction may be inbuilt
but if there were no wars
would soldiers after all be soldiers?

# THE TACTICS OF WAR

National boundaries made us unique.
Belonging to one nation but made of different tribes
different ethnicities
different beliefs
We all lived together peacefully
Our enemies, if any, were those outside far away
who may want to hurt us

Within our own boundaries we were safe
Then we woke up one day
and found that war had changed tactics
We fight and kill each other
we are refugees in our land
Our children played together in the streets
went to each other's birthday parties
supported each other.

Today, bewildered, they ask why they can't
play with Hindus or Muslims or Christians
why Serbians are not friends anymore with Albanians
And why Hutus and Tutsis are frightened of each other
How do we answer?
What do we tell them?

That war has changed its tactics
and we do not know who our enemies are any more
Those we used to call outsiders have come to help us.
People we've never heard of have sent us
food and clothing and medicines.
We used to feel safe in our own nation
but not anymore.

War has changed tactics
we are refugees in our own land.
Our homes plundered and burnt down
by those we called neighbours.
Now we know we have better neighbours
in the world outside
than those who live next door.
Why has war changed tactics so?

# WHY DID IT HAPPEN TO US?

Sunshine and rain
heat and cold
calm and storm
deserts and forests
parched earth and swamps
lakes and rivers
sunshine and rain
tears and sorrow
laughter and joy
Dwellers on earth experience these
Summer and Winter
Spring and Autumn

Frost, snow and ice
temperatures below freezing
hailstones, thunder, lightning
rain and more rain
floods, hurricanes, earthquakes
cyclones, tornadoes, volcanoes
icebergs, sinking ships
drought, heat waves
forest fires, parched earth
no water, no food
starvation, thirst and death

Why did it happen to us?
Sunshine and rain
laughter, joy
Singing and dancing
sorrow, deep sorrow
heartache, hopelessness and depression

One day is different to the other
One nation's calamities different from the other
Somehow life goes on and we grow old and die
Hard to accept that it happens
to some people and in other places
We are exempt

Then we wake up and the fallen trees tell us a story
A devastation!
A hurricane while we slept
We look around, it has happened to us!
Why us? It always happened to other people
Do we accept, do we deny or find an explanation?

No!
We get angry, very angry and sad that it happened to us
Then we ask questions
questions that have no answers
questions like, why did it happen to us?
then the answer comes from all around the world

Why did it happen to us?
We stand amazed at the answer
which is like an echo of the question we asked
We are surprised that others ask the same questions
and we thought it was alright if it happened to them
and not to us
Could it be that others like us feel pain?
And extreme weather conditions?

That even though they live in cold countries
they must feel cold
Could it be that those who live in hot countries
feel the heat?
Sunshine and rain
heat and cold
calm and storm
Hailstones, thunder, volcanoes
icebergs, sinking ships
Winter, Summer, Spring and Autumn

Why did it happen to us?
Love, laughter, joy, great joy
tragic accidents, terminal illness
separation, loneliness then death
Sorrow deep, sorrow no one understands,
bereavement, isolation, depression
Funny old world.
Why did it happen to us?

We come together not to mock,
not to laugh but to love
embrace and comfort each other
only when we realize that it happens to all of us
because we all feel pain
feel cold and heat
love and heartache
tears and sorrow
but we do not know why it happens to us.

# THANKS FOR THROWING AWAY
# THE KNIFE

I left the world
I lived in the world without being a part of it
I left the world
did the best I could to those I came in contact with
cried with those who cried
laughed with those who laughed
that was how I lived

I lived in the world without being a part of it
I left the world
There was so much that created discourse and distaste
their playground was covered in blood
their laughter was over dead bodies
When they appeared happy
it was because they had wounded and hurt someone
That was why I lived in the world
and could not be a part of it
I left the world

There was a change I had to go through
a change that changed me
a change to make me like them
Spill blood on the playground
and laugh at the dead bodies
It makes no difference, they said
they are dead and will not hear you

I could not be changed
So I left the world
I threw away the knife
to live a better life
and shed no blood

*Dedicated to those who had the courage to leave gangs
and get a good education.*

# A BETTER LIFE

Generations change and adapt to the world they live in
So much is assumed but the experience is so different
The willingness to learn and understand
leads through a path of humility
It abandons assumption and throws light on reality
The desire for change in most people's lives
is for the better
Even those who abandon riches to live a simple life
are looking for something which makes them feel better

Mankind has travelled a long way
from the time they lived in caves
and fought with sharp stones and clubs
to a place where they dream
of expanding their domains to other planets
The dream for a better world
is birthed by the imperfection we see around us
the decay and misery, the poverty and injustice
Men and women have migrated
from towns, villages, cities and nations
to find that 'better life' which sometimes chides us all
for with every 'better life'
comes its own unique problems

When children resolve to build a better life
than what their parents had they do well
However if their resolve is born of resentment
which is due to a lack of understanding
they sometimes come against
what they resented in their own lives
Dreams and aspirations are powerful
They spur us on to achieve greater things
if in humility we recognise
that failures are but challenges
we learn to overcome

Where we are right now is not perfect
but it is better than where we were
There is always room for improvement
on what already exists
We quit trying when we are tired
but the best time to quit
is when we are content with our lot
Contentment is the highest achievement in life
It does not wish for what others have
It does not resent what it has
Beautiful contentment, living at peace with oneself
That is wealth!

# THE DARKNESS OF WAR

It is not the sound of gunfire
It is not the explosion of bombs
It is not the wailing of mothers for their sons
nor the silent stooped walk of the grey headed man
bearing the grief of his son lost in action
It is not the knock on the door to break the news
to a young wife and bewildered children
that is private grief which cannot be shared
It is not the victory parades of those who won
nor the subdued retreat of the defeated army
It is the darkness that covers all our hearts
when we hear and watch the news
 of those killed in action
whether they are our enemies
or our own men and women

# AFTER THE FIRE

Invisible to the eye the tiny green shoots
push their way upwards
to reclaim what is rightfully theirs
after the fire
For miles nothing could be seen but
blackened earth and charred trees
some lying where they fell, now turned to charcoal
The grey spots in between are but ashes
Hopelessness and heartbreak for the lush green forest
with its enviable variety of wild life

How someone's mistake and carelessness could
cause a forest to disappear is sad
The smoke formed a thick cloud and draped
the sky with the same blackness
as if in mourning with the earth
As the days turned to weeks the rain clouds
unable to hold their grief emptied themselves to
soothe, comfort and cleanse the wounds
of the blackened earth

And the earth opening herself up received comfort
from each healing drop of rain into her very heart
The hidden seeds responded sending tiny shoots up
dotting the blackened earth like the stubble
of an unshaven man in the morning
Growing slowly but surely to reclaim the land
where generations of their ancestors stood
in beauty and majesty

# AND HE SAID TO ME

And He said to me
*Those who rise from the ashes*
*will never be put down again.*
I sought to understand the world
it was a mess before I arrived
There had been two world wars
slavery and the holocaust
all before I was born.

Countless wars
exploitation of the weak by the strong
and the poor by the rich.
Somehow it was as if man made a world
in which there was not enough of anything.
One part of the world seems to have all they could wish

for while the other part starved to death.
the blindness that afflicted the hearts of men
made some of them believe it was fine
to take what belonged to others
and yet refuse to give
even the crumbs of what they had taken
to the starving poor.
Food wasted and thrown away
while a few doors down the road
someone went to bed on an empty stomach

The thinking is wrong
the belief is wrong
 the weather is wrong
and now the climate is changing
not only because we have not taken care of our
environment
but primarily because we have not taken care of each
other
The trees are unhappy
the clouds weep until the rivers overflow with their tears
Somehow people remember to care again
helping each other through the flood waters
not knowing that the clouds wept
at the lack of care we have shown each other

We drop bombs
kill the innocent to punish the guilty
accuse God when the hurricane hits and the earth quakes
bringing devastation just like the bombs we dropped
killing the innocent as well as the guilty
Then we rise
somehow we rise
dusting off the ashes
and washing away the mud
What have we learned?

# BECAUSE IT IS RIGHT FOR RIGHT
# TO SPEAK LOUD AND CLEAR

When we see wrong exposed
in the lives of those in positions of trust
does the world fall apart?
Do we lose trust and respect for humanity?

When wrong has looked so right
and excuses are presented as reasons for injustice
those who question or oppose the excuses
are regarded as enemies
Is it really impossible for some people
to live right and do right?

How can they live right
and walk hand-in-hand with wrong?
How can they refuse to speak
against the injustice of sexual exploitation?

Nobody is perfect, they say
so those in positions of trust throw caution to the wind
and wallow in the mire
A day of reckoning is sure to come to all
a day when right looks us in the face
and reason refuses to justify excuses
Gifts may entice the naive and vulnerable
The trap becomes a stronghold
It doesn't matter who gets hurt

The perpetrators of sexual injustice
may think it feels right
until right refuses to be silenced any more by excuses
because it is right for right to speak out
loud and clear

Right is right
Wrong is wrong
for every person on the planet
whatever their position in life

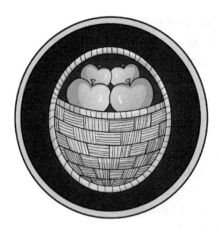

# Chapter 4
# Attention Please, Attention Please!

# A CRY FOR ADOPTION

You can stop my tears
You can ease my pain
You can step into my life and make it different
You can stop the tears and ease the pain
You know you can
You can bring me home to where you are
You can show me the love
that I have so far only dreamed about

You can stop my tears
You can ease my pain
You can take me into your arms and make me yours
You can stop my tears
I have lived in homes
homes which never belonged to me
I have lived with parents
foster parents
When I began to feel love and security
they moved me on

Unless you step into my life
and make me yours, completely yours
I will never know what love is
I dream of a home
a permanent home
with lots of love and laughter
of a Mum and Dad
though not my own I can call my own
and they can call me their own

You are that Mum
You are that Dad
who can stop my tears and ease my pains
You can make my dreams come true
You can stop my tears

*This poem is written and dedicated to Paddy, Steven and
Hilary Taylor of Telford.*

# ATTENTION PLEASE, ATTENTION PLEASE!

It is a busy rushing world of men, women and children
Everyone a destination in mind, a bus or train to catch
The shout of *Attention please*! *Attention please*!
seems to go unnoticed
because the shout is not made by mouth and voice

The shout is in the eyes of those the mad rush has left
behind
They stand on street corners, at our bus and train stations
They sleep in the underpass, on pavements
or wherever the night falls on them

They are shouting to us, to you and to me
*Attention please! Attention please!*
"I have lost my way in life"
Why do we walk on as though blind?
Why do we avoid them?
Rushing as if time itself would disappear
if we stopped

Whose sons are they?
Whose daughters?
Whose fathers?
Whose mothers?
Their tears are not seen on the outside
They weep in their hearts, their souls
In their eyes, they shout to us

*Attention please! Attention please!*
"I have lost my way in life
Won't you help me?"

# THE GRAVEYARD

The graveyard is silent but birds still sing in the trees and the bees buzz over the flowers. There is life in the graveyard, the resting place for when our life's work is done. It is good to know that there is a place where our loved ones can lay us to rest and return home to get on with their lives.

The funeral service is for the dead to be laid to rest. Coming to terms with the death of a loved one does not begin at the funeral service. Years and months must pass when each special and precious moment is relived, sometimes bringing tears, in our memories.

How special it is to read about great works done centuries ago. How they shine!

Funerals are not an end in themselves. They simply set the stage for our memory to relish, or abhor, what has been done by the dead.

A lesson for every living person to remember is our deeds do not die with us. They either shine or bring shame. They serve as an example or a warning for us all.

Every life serves as a lesson.

# HE WAITED

Starved, malnourished, emaciated
A ghost of a person
barely alive
staggers on, eyes glazed
looks into the distance, but eyes see nothing
Miles of dry earth which look like a desert

He waits in hope, double hope
whether it be death that ends this life of misery
or human help to nourish his body back to health
he stands in the middle of two possibilities
Choice is a luxury he can't afford
He just waits

There is no strength in him to fight
even the flies
They could be excused to think they are sitting on a
corpse
He stands there, ribs visible under his skin
eyes sunken, mouth dried
He looks out to the distance but sees nothing
At this point food would taste like sand in his mouth

Taste buds no longer respond to the smell of food
Hunger deprives him of sleep
lips cracked and sore
no sense of smell
living in the twilight of death
He hears human voices in the distance
like a dream
he hallucinates
sees faces of loved ones

He sits himself gently on the ground
and leans against a tree
He is gone
He joins those who are free from earthly misery
The human voices he had heard were from those who
had come to help
Help came too late
He is gone
He is free, even from the flies

Some are still waiting

*This poem is dedicated to the victims of famine*

# THE POWER OF THE CREDITOR

*The creditor has come to take my sons to be slaves*
*(2 Kings 4:1)*

The creditor, he credits for power.
His credit to you is the power he has over you, and all
you possess
The power of the creditor can make you his slave
though you are the son of a prophet
and though you fear the Lord
The creditor comes, and in him there is no mercy,
no fear of the Lord
His only fear is to lose his power
So your sons he will take
and slaves of them he will make
though they are the sons of a prophet

The power of the creditor
has it changed since the days of Elisha?
The creditor today gives you a card
with which you may purchase whatever you wish
The limit of credit he increases
He knows the more he gives
the less you are able to resist
Soon the time comes
Very often it is when he knows you cannot repay
what you have borrowed
He strikes with no mercy, no pity

Your sons he will take and slaves of them he will make
His power will repossess your home
make you bankrupt
It was all in the small print you never bothered to read
The power of the creditor.
Many have fallen when his power he wields
His victims include the nobles of every class and clan

Run to the man of God and cry to him for deliverance
He looks at you in pity
and asks "What have you got in your house?"
Nothing, it seems, except a little pot of oil
but with it God can turn back
both the fury and power of the creditor.

God can use the most insignificant things we possess
to bring deliverance in a time of need
When God asked Moses, "What is in your hand?"
Moses had no idea that the piece of dried wood
he was using as a shepherd's staff
could be used to bring a powerful nation to its knees

God's love and graciousness pardons us and delivers us
from those whose power always makes us slaves
What have you got in your house?
What is in your hand?
God can and will use the things we scorn
to be the instruments of our freedom.

Have you known the power of the creditor?
Have you known the power of God to deliver?

# THE LUXURY TO LINGER

The designer of our bodies commands us to rest, and give our thoughts a rest, so that He can replenish and heal our hurting minds and refresh our souls for each coming week. Somehow spending a day in a week doing nothing but listening to God's word is unthinkable in our world today.

A friend once said that she needed a holiday to recover from her holiday. Being busy and doing something all the time soon saps the energy from us. Taking time off in whatever form is still filled with other activities which leave us more exhausted.

Take another look at your life; give yourself time to think about the things which cause stress. Do you have the luxury to linger and appreciate the flowers? On a conveyor belt there is no luxury to linger. Pick up what you need before it disappears.

When you finish eating the luxury to linger seems a crime when there is a queue of people waiting to be seated. The rush of life is everywhere; the pause button seems to have been damaged, and to stop you have to be rich enough to choose where to eat and have a table booked before you arrive.

Time for a break from work? Even for a short break you have to work on the conveyor belt for long hours to save up the money you need for a break. And when you return the conveyor belt awaits to suck up every ounce of energy restored to you.

Life is not meant to be like that: We made it so. No other commandment is broken more than the Third Commandment.

To think that God had to put a time of rest in the commandments for us to remember to keep it holy. We think it is another rule to obey or break or simply ignore, but it is the one rule which tells us to STOP! Stop and rest. Give the cow, sheep and goat a rest! Give everything rest, even your thoughts. Could we try to rest one day a week?

# READ THE SIGNS!

Some people no longer read the signs. They assume it will be as it has always been. They stumble through life when they fail to read the signs.

They don't read the labels so they wash their clothes at the wrong temperature. They hand-wash clothes which should be dry-cleaned. In anger and frustration, they blame everybody else but themselves.

A young man stood pushing a door to open, lost his temper and kicked the door through because he thought that someone had locked him out. Refusing to understand that he had to pay for the broken door, he was taken to court. Unfortunately for him, there was a sign above the door which read PULL TO OPEN. The young man has always known to push doors open so he did not read the sign. He pushed and pushed, got frustrated and kicked the door through.

What if he did not have the strength to kick the door through? He would have walked away and never entered a building where doors are to be pulled open. Life is like that. When we push where we should pull doors remain closed, and when we pull when we should push we may walk away from something we should have had.

PLEASE READ THE SIGN! READ THE LABEL!

# THE PAPER GENERATION

The silver is out of fashion
the china has no place
even glass has become expensive
Paper rules
from the cups to the plates
from tablecloths to napkins
King Paper has saved the day

This generation has all the time
to enjoy parties and fast food.
but no time to wash and dry dishes
Why should dishes be washed
and silver polished?
Why risk all the hazards of broken china?
Paper rules

Think about the planet,
think about recycling,
spare a thought for the trees
from which you get your paper.
Think, think, and think again of paper and how it feels
Is it good only because it can be thrown away?
Recycled perhaps?
But where is the care?
Why does paper feel used and abused?
Here today, gone tomorrow
That is paper

Paper used to have pride of place
It gathered dust
but it was cared for
Carefully and beautifully arranged on bookshelves
Generations opened it with care
It preserved stories, history,
geography and the Holy Script.
That was paper
Now it is no longer fun
and there is no pride in being paper
Books are on screens
Money is in plastic cards
Cups and plates and table cloths
are the descendents of good old paper
Let us not abuse an old friend

# BEAUTIFUL BUT EMPTY

The photographs and paintings hang on the wall
the dining table laid up
as though dinner was to be served
the book shelves stocked books on every subject
This was a house I would never have entered
its grounds viewed and admired from afar
I may have had the privilege
to glance the occupants as they passed by
Today the beautiful mansion stands empty
With a sum of money I can join the teaming crowds
who like me are fascinated by the sheer luxury
in which some have lived in the past
makes me wonder how many beautiful homes today
would stand empty for those who will come after
to admire what we all must leave behind some day
though today we are fenced in from the crowd

# WHAT IS YOUR POSTCODE?

Where do you live?

What is your address and postcode?

Do you live in a world where you are loved because you deserve to be loved, or do you live in the kingdom of God where you are loved even though you do not deserve it?

Where do you live? Do you live in a world where you are judged before you do any wrong or do you live in the kingdom of God where salvation abounds to the worst of sinners?

There are two places you could live, even here and now. You can move house and change your postcode. Your life will reflect your address and postcode. The grace and peace you experience will bear witness to where you live.

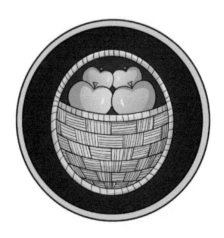

# Chapter 5
# Purpose

# A PEN THAT DOESN'T WRITE

A pen that doesn't write?
What is the purpose of a pen that doesn't write?
Whatever its brand name
or if it were gold- or silver-plated
and packaged in the best of boxes
I have no patience for a pen that doesn't write
for what purpose is it to carry it about
when it cannot perform a simple task
like signing a signature?

For me a pen must write
That is the whole purpose of it
What was I created for?
What is my purpose on earth?
What are the jobs I was created to do?
I collect pens
but I am not a collector of pens for fun
I like to write and any pen will do
only if it does what it was made for
Oh that I may know what my purpose on earth is
so that I do not take up space
just to be added to the numbers in a census

I like to think I was made for a purpose
When that purpose calls do I respond?
And does my response fulfil
the purpose for which I was created?
I do not wish to live a life empty of passion and purpose
like a pen that doesn't write

# STAGNANT WATER

There is something so refreshing and fragrant
about running water in a stream or river
Running water renews itself constantly flowing
Stagnant water is not like that
Any movement seen on it
is but gentle ripples created by the wind
Greenish brown, it is full of dead leaves
and other things unimaginable
Stagnant water goes nowhere
refreshes no one
not even the ducks who may use it
simply because it is there

# FISHING

Lazy work is it?
Throwing out the fishing line
to sit and wait
Waiting for "tug tug"
a sign to pull

The fishing rod catches nothing
unless there is bait attached to it
usually something the fish likes
You may not like maggots
but if that is what the fish likes
then you may as well get used to handling maggots

Sitting and waiting
as more hooked maggots are tossed into the pond
you hope that the fish will be attracted
to the maggot at the end of your fishing line

Patience and hope at work
for you to sit and wait
try and try again
and be willing to try yet again
until the fish takes a shine
to that one maggot
at the end of your fishing line

# MOST PEOPLE KNOW WHAT THEY WANT IN LIFE

Be at peace with yourself
Most people know what they want in life
but few are willing to achieve what they want
When they do
they need all the courage and determination it takes
to achieve it
What are the goals you have set for your life?
Are they achievable?
Have you got the resources?
Do you know someone who can help you
or point you in the right direction?
Are you focused enough not to be distracted
when interruptions come your way?
Are you able to handle them
so you could go back to what you were doing before?

When halfway to your dream
you find that it is a mistake
that it is not achievable
or that it is more a fantasy than a reality
Are you humble enough to admit it to yourself?
Will you be able to take on something less glamorous
but within your strength?
Can you be true to yourself
when everyone thinks you should be different?

Knowing and appreciating yourself goes a long way
If you do not appreciate your strengths and weaknesses
you allow people to put on you loads you cannot carry
Or they will pull you down
and make of you some kind of doormat
Know the difference
and be at peace with yourself

# TRANSIENT AND TEMPORAL

Transient and temporal
That is how I feel
Everywhere and every place the feeling remains
Transient and temporal
Is there a place?
Will there ever be a place of settling down?
Of feeling at home?
A place to belong, to be a part of?
Or is all this earthly existence only meant to be
transient and temporal?
Fifty years have passed
As I travel to places and see faces
I wonder if they all feel the same

I heard the young couple talk about how long it took
to clear their grandparents' house and put it up for sale
They had a lot of stuff that would fetch a fortune.
The house, if only it was in a good location
would have sold for more
As they talked and made their plans,
transient and temporal was not on their minds,
not for them anyway,
for their grandparents maybe
since they have graciously passed on
and left them a fortune.

I wondered how long it would be before they too
started feeling transient and temporal
laying up treasures for generations unborn
hoping that life would be a bit more comfortable
for descendants they would not see
No treasure laid is for ourselves
though for a season we may enjoy their benefits

# DOES LOVE BLINDFOLD US?

Like a young plant growing
from the stock of an old tree
life continues to the next generation
Must all life begin and end
with so much left undone?

And a hundred years from now
will there still be homeless people
and those who give up on life?

Why is that we are unable to learn
and improve on what has been?
Why do people who fall in love abuse their partners?
They walk down the aisle and say "I do"
only to fight and quarrel
until they feel more like strangers than lovers
as though they were aliens from outer space

Does life blindfold us when we are born
so we repeat the mistakes our parents made?
Why does it still hurt to love?
Why do lovers break each other's hearts?
Is there a way to find peace in our hearts
and make love and laughter part of each passing day?

# HAVE YOU EVER BEEN YOUNG?

Have you ever been young?
And did you not think that you could change the world?
Did you not think that older people were slow
and a little out of date?
Did you not find that the world
was ruled by all the wrong people?

And did you as a young man
not feel a right to at least approach every beautiful girl
as though they were all made just for you?

As a young woman
were you not attracted to a man
only by his looks and how he spoke?

Have you ever been young?
Did you not think you had answers
to what most people got wrong?
You were daring and took chances
which makes you shudder today

The years have knocked sense into you
you now seem more articulate and thoughtful
you now appreciate that there are things you can change
while accepting and tolerating
those things you have no control over.

Yet do you appoint yourself
as judge and jury of the young?
Are you quick to condemn and even suppress
the energy and enthusiasm that remind you
of your own youthful foolishness?

Have you ever been young?
Then you will know that the fire of youth
cannot be quenched
It needs gentle but firm leadership
That brings the best out of our young people
Soon they too will learn with time and years
to appreciate the things that they cannot change
and change what they can

It is their right because they are young

# QUIET

I need to find a place of quiet retreat
a place of solitude
a place I can be alone with myself
and nature is a kind and gentle companion

A quiet walk in the forest
when the sun is most harsh and hot
A peaceful walk by the lake
when the dawn breaks into day
A stroll in the garden
when the sun slips quietly behind the hills
kissing all nature good night.

I need to be alone in the night
where crickets chirp, owls hoot
and the moonlight dances gently on the lake
Then myself and I can have a quiet talk
of things that have gone by
and things that are new
when I have spent this time with myself
I can walk into the future
and share life with friends who care.

# SCRAP METAL DEALER

Like a scrap metal dealer
he picks up what people throw away
To them it is of no use
but He knows something good
will come out of what has been thrown away
He picks up all the junk and broken pieces
which seem to have no use

He puts them together
Some He re-shapes
Others He melts down
When His work is done
He uses the recycled material
from the junk which has been discarded

Our lives can be full of junk
the junk of hurtful feelings
of bitterness, anger, envy and denied forgiveness
The scrap metal dealer picks us up
He starts His work of cleaning us
melting us down
and reshaping us into brand new people
who can love and laugh again
He even makes us able to cry
when hurts have hardened our hearts

Looking back we learn
when the mangled pieces
have been re-shaped and melted down
that we are loved
Broken relationships can be mended
 if we are willing to forgive those who hurt us
The scrap metal dealer picks up all the old things
and makes them new

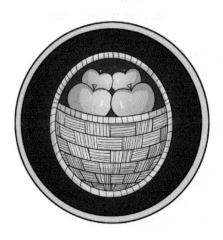

# Chapter 6
# The Love That Causes Pain

# WHY DOES WISDOM COME SO LATE?

Why are we wise only with hindsight?
After the years of foolishness
have robbed us of all that is precious
why does wisdom come so late?
Why did we never see the good in each other
when everything was going so well with us?
What made us think
that somehow time was our possession
that we were in some control of the events of our lives?
Why did we let a life so precious
slip through our fingers?
Why does wisdom come so late?
It seems as though life itself has passed us by
the things we could have done
the joys we could have shared
Now they all seem to be locked away
somewhere in the past among treasures unclaimed
and the future bids us be quiet
as in silence we reflect
on hard lessons life has taught us.
Why does wisdom come so late?

# THE LOVE THAT CAUSES PAIN

I don't know, but the love that causes pain has had its day with me.

I look to the Love that accepts me just as I am, and by its own power, transforms me into what I can never be without it.

I do not change to adapt myself to this Love; this Love changes me and adapts me to itself.

This is the Love that sought me through pain – can I resist it?

This is the Love that first of all sought me when there was nothing about me worthy of acceptance.

I was yet in sin and did not know my need for a Saviour.

Yes! He sought me because of His great love for me
And His love causes no pain.

# I HAD TO GO AWAY

I had to go away
and leave it all behind
It was killing me
Travel to the moon I might have done
to Mars, Jupiter or Venus
where I could be alone among the stars
but the stars do not come down to earth
and a rocket I did not have.

So I had to go away
and leave it all behind
to stay alive

Now I am back and what good it has done to me?
To look again at the dust that claimed all you had?
Picking up the pieces I build myself a new life
The memories remain but life must change

Yet love remains bright as the stars above
for me to look and wonder at the diamond in the sky

# THERE IS SO MUCH YOU WILL NEVER KNOW

There is so much you will never know
so it should remain
my secret to keep
but not from him who sees all things
knows all things and sustains us all

The comfort to know that I have never been alone
and that you too were held close to his heart
This is where we rest
in Him
privileged to travel with the gentle companion
who knows just how to
keep safe those who trust in Him

There is no need for you to know
about half the pain I have been through
the anguish, the tears
a privilege to experience something
so wholesome and consuming
It killed the child in me
and released a woman willing to be a child again
willing to learn to live and love again
willing to be led by him who knows all things
sees all things and sustains us all
there is so much you will never know

So it should remain
my secret treasured and shared with Him alone
My gentle companion
whose whispers drown the noise of the world
and gives laughter in the rain of tears
If it sounds crazy
remember He was also called a mad man

# OUR PLEDGE

Our pledge was so that we will live
loving each other for the rest of our lives
in the safety of knowing we belong only to each other

Our pledge was so that we will work hard
at making our love last as long as we live
so that the sweetness we have known will not turn sour

Our pledge was so that no one will come between us
That was our pledge

Our pledge was to have and to hold
until death do us part
so what happened to our pledge?
Why am I so alone?
Why do I feel as though part of me has died?

You have found real happiness, you say
 in another woman's arms
You are in love, you tell me
you even want me to be happy for you
so what was it we had
when we pledged our love for each other?

What was it we found
when we walked hand in hand
in the days when you said you'd die
if I ever changed my mind?
What was it, my love, what was it?

You say you are leaving
I am sure you tell her now
all the things you used to tell me
when you thought you loved me
I don't know what happened

All I know is that I pledged my love to you
 and I wish to hold it true to the end
though now you may well indeed have found true love

Now it is no longer 'our pledge' as it is 'my pledge'
If I could fall in love again with someone else,
 if I could feel the way I felt
when you first took me in your arms
if I could
I would not
because I know I pledged  my love to you


(*Dedicated to Joyce*)

# NO ONE CAN HURT MORE

No one can hurt more than those you love
No one can break your heart more
than the one you gave your heart to
No one can make you more angry
as you lie awake at night
than the one you trusted most
That is why He taught us to forgive
He knows too well how we can all hurt each other
He knows also that forgiveness heals
both the one who is hurt
and those who have caused such pain
Forgiveness heals the soul
Sometimes it is hard to forgive
when we forget that we too are capable of causing pain
The jar from which God pours
His healing oil of forgiveness
remains sealed
until we forgive those who hurt us
When we do
God pours His healing oil into those jars
so we can apply them to our bleeding hearts
He will help us forgive those who sin against us
even those who hurt us most

# DROWNED IN AN OCEAN OF LOVE SONGS

Drowned in an ocean of love songs
Buried under an avalanche of icy cold silence
until He touched my body dead and frozen
and healed the cuts and bruises
He made me whole

Now I sing and listen only to songs
that speak of His love
Now I avoid the songs that drain the soul
I choose not to wait any longer
when your silence freezes to ice
I keep on the move
I sing songs of His love and keep on the move

You must have good reasons to be the way you are
You may even think it was all some kind of joke
In the end we become part of a people
who find it difficult to connect and take blame
a people who must always present themselves
to be in right

I know I must be wrong
but I am not afraid to be
So I keep on the move
to avoid the love songs that drown the soul

I keep on the move
away from your silence
which you have every reason on earth to keep

Some of us live real lives
so we make mistakes
and that is okay
Some of us experience hurts which make us angry
but we keep moving on

# FAR AWAY

Far away, so far away as it should be
No memories no encounter just far away
It is a choice we both made to be so near
and yet far away
So you may walk down my street
you may even knock on my door
but you will be as far away as you have always been
When you chose to be a stranger
almost as though from another planet
I chose to be a child of the earth
Here I remain a child of the earth at home
always at home where I belong
Even though you chose to be far away

# I DON'T WANT TO GO BACK

I don't want to go back
I want to go forward
I want to walk away from all the things that held me
back
I wish to think that things could be better
than they have been
It is when we look back and feel bad
for all the wrong things that have hurt me
that I can walk away

It is going to be hard work I know
I  must work hard on myself
not to fall back into bitterness and hatred and fighting
I need to work hard against the suspicions
and lack of trust I have for poeple

Building is hard work
It is easier to knock down what has been built
than build something new
We all need to build something good
for the generations to come

Some people believe that the world
will never be a better place
that we will always fight and bomb each other
If there are a few people
who will choose to believe the opposite
I would like to join them

If a handful of people believe in the positive
we can stand up and challenge the negative
We need to make this world a better place
Yes, remember the wrong things
Only so that we will not repeat them
They should challenge us
to turn things around for the better
If we are willing to try
even to take one small step
we will surprise ourselves at what we can do.

# TO LIVE WITHOUT TRUST IS TO DIE

Many of us need a human presence, a human touch, a human voice. We need to see a human face, a human smile communicating eye to eye. Listening, watching, and coming to an agreement or even to a disagreement. It is all part of being human.

To be locked away from humanity is to lose our own humanity. A life without trust is a cruel prison which suffocates and destroys its victims. Reaching out, giving people a second chance, drawing out buried treasure from those who have forgotten to trust.

Is like bringing to life something which was dead.

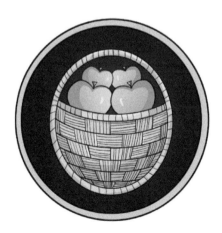

# Chapter 7
# Stay in Touch

# STAY IN TOUCH

You've grown and left home.
You are your own man.
You travel the world,
choose your friends,
date the girls.
But I still want to know where you are.
How are you? Are you well?
Stay in touch.

You have left our home but not our hearts
You don't hold my hand anymore
But in a way you do
Your hand on a telephone, my hands on the receiver
We speak as though we hold hands again
when you stay in touch

In your voice I can tell
that your hands are trembling
You don't have to tell me
she is right there by your side
You have found her at last, darling
Well done
We wish you both well
Now that you have found her
will you please not forget to stay in touch?

# KEEP PRAYING

Keep praying
There is nothing to lose
The situation is hopeless
That is when we need to pray most
When there seems to be no answer
it seems foolish to pray
Every evidence is to the contrary.
But faith He said is the evidence
of things hoped for
the substance of things not seen
So keep praying

Remember Elijah
He kept praying when the
sky was blue with never
a single cloud in sight
He kept praying till only a cloud
as big as a man's hand appeared

Keep praying
and look for the slightest sign He gives you
then praise God for his faithfulness
Faith has always looked foolish
The old book has records to show
he prayed for fire, that holy man Elijah
after he drenched the sacrifice in water
making it impossible to burn
to show that the lord God specialises in impossibilities

He prayed for the rain when there was no sign of rain
Can we believe and pray like him?
The old book tells us that he was a man just like us
but he prayed

So keep praying
until the answer comes through
Remember an answer is not always "yes"
Keep praying till you have heard him say
"yes" or "no" or "wait"
Keep praying

# GUARDING THE HEART

It is good that the heart be settled, so that peace like a river can flow unhindered toward eternity. Appreciating the journey from where He first took us, where we are now and where He is taking us, so that our lives are not just a series of events.

To know that we are on a journey which ends in eternity puts meaning into everything which happens to us. Responding not in the heat of those things which are unpleasant but resting in the knowledge that even the unpleasant things have purpose.

We may not be able to change the way other people think and behave, but we can be an influence. We can refuse to react in the way they expect us to. It can be a hard journey because the battle we fight is within. When we are no longer controlled by self will, when we feel the first signs of anger, hurt and resentment rising up within us, remember that "he who controls his spirit is greater than he who conquers a city".

It is good that the heart be established and settled so that peace will flow through us to others.

What a responsibility it is, but it does not come cheap. It is when we work on ourselves and allow the word of God to dwell in us that our lives can reflect the beauty of the Lord.

"Work out your own salvation with fear and trembling, for it is God who is at work in you both to will and to do His good pleasure."

It is his good pleasure that the heart be established, "guard your heart with all diligence for out of it flows the issues of life".

"Out of the abundance of the mouth speaks", this means that I speak from whatever it is I have stored in my heart. If my heart is not filled with peace, I cannot speak peace to myself or anyone and there is much in the world to stir up resentment and anger if we do not guard our hearts.

# CAST ALL YOUR BURDENS UPON HIM FOR HE CARES FOR YOU

Looks like the perfect message to the weak, the feeble and the lazy: to have someone on whom we can throw our burdens and live a 'good life' with no burdens at all. It sounds wonderful.

To be able to carry burdens is a sign of strength: strong people like to carry their burdens and sometimes even the burdens of other people! Some burdens are so heavy to carry that we leave them in the way to make others trip and fall over them.

There are two things we can do with burdens, carry them ourselves or throw them on Him who is strong enough to carry the sins of all mankind. He always waits for us to throw or give to Him those things we are unable to cope with. He does not snatch them from our hands but waits for us to give them to Him.

Sometimes we carry burdens until we reach breaking point before we are willing to give them to Him. Other times we are foolish enough to allow ourselves to be crushed before we call on Him.

What is a burden? A burden is anything which makes our lives shift from normality.

It could be a good thing which consumes our energy, or a bad thing which may not look much but can shift our lives from what we call normal and steal our joy and peace.

# FADING HOPE

The hope I had in any person fades so quickly
My plans come tumbling down
then I turn around to seek Him
who alone has endless supplies and endless provisions
The rarest commodity on earth
which is steadfast love
never ceases in His kingdom

His mercies never come to an end
They are new every morning
Let me live in this kingdom
Let me have this faith
not in man whose supplies can run dry
and whose fortune can be stolen
but in Him who knows my needs before I pray
In Him who has plans for my good
my God in whom I trust

# ENDLESS SUPPLIES

Endless supplies and endless provisions
as each day begins His endless supplies remain
never exhausted
never running dry
 release me from the fear that grips men's hearts
of sudden collapse
and disappearance of fortunes stored or hoarded.
Which thieves can break in and steal
moths and rust can corrupt precious goods
Financial institutions collapse
banks fail and businesses fold

The great man who promised me so much died yesterday
the executors of his fortunes have other plans
which don't include me.
But I know of one whose supplies never run dry.

# THE BREAD OF LIFE

With expectation, the crowd waited for the verdict
It was the best meal cooked by the best chef
People travelled from far and near
to taste this amazing meal

The young woman who came as a tourist
was asked to work for a day with the chef
When asked what she thought of the food
she said that she did not know
"What do you mean you do not know?"
asked a reporter keen to write an article
about the food everyone was talking about
"Well," she said
pausing as if to find the right words
"It is ok and all the ingredients are alright sort of"

The crowd listened
disbelieving what they heard
It transpired that instead of working with the chef
she was busy looking around the magnificent kitchen
tasting food which someone had brought to the kitchen

It is no wonder that she had so little to say
about the food she had tasted
It was not the food the chef had cooked

Have we indeed tasted the bread of life?
Or have we just eaten any old bread?

# FAITH

A day comes when it all becomes plain, every doubt dispelled and faith strengthened. Faith after all is meant to be our travel companion in the dark, when we are made to hold the hand we cannot see.

Faith is a journey through life when nothing makes sense except what we have dared to believe. As we journey on, the light shines to brighten the darkness doubt inflicts on us until daylight breaks to confirm what we believed along the way.

Then humility comes to clothe us as those who have had a travelling companion in the dark passages of life, and have believed that what He said is true.

# TEST FOR PEACE

Let us test for peace in all the things we do and allow in our lives. He called us to peace

He left with us His peace.

In tribulations He commands us to be of good cheer for He sees that it will be our lot in the world, the world he has overcome.

How comforting to know that this menacing world has been overcome by Him.

It is like saying – look this world is never going to overcome you. You will have tribulation but you can laugh at it all. Why? Because I have overcome it. I have got it in my power it is in my hands, so do not give the tribulations a second thought. It must be so; the world will give tribulations to all who follow the Master who overcame it.

That is why He leaves us peace which the world cannot give. In fact it is doubtful if the world has any peace at all.

# SOMETIMES ALL YOU CAN DO IS...

Sometimes, all you can do is put the sacrifice on the wood. When the wood has been out in the rain and it is wet, there will be nothing much you can do about it but wait for the impossible to happen.

Wet wood never burned easily; sometimes wet wood never burned at all. Dry wood never burned without fire – on its own, dry wood simply remained dry.

If there was a fire about, dry wood would burn to ashes long before wet wood caught a whiff of smoke.

So why did Elijah wet the sacrifice and the wood? Why was it as if he was deliberately making it harder, even impossible, for the wood to burn? Was he trying to make a representation of what the people of Israel had become? Was he, in doing so, echoing the situation around him; showing how impossible it seemed for God to have relevance in the lives of a people who have exchanged their God for the gods of wood and stone?

Remember the prophets of Baal had laid their sacrifice on dry wood, and though they did their very best to call on their god, nothing happened.

So, it could be that Elijah was simply making a bad situation worse.

Then the fire came down and burned the wet sacrifice and the wet wood, and also licked up the water in the trenches around the alter.

God was in effect telling them that no matter how impossible their situation seemed, He was still God and therefore able to revive what had become dead and wet. He was able to allow his fire to burn in the coldest of hearts.

So those who had never seen their God who is a consuming fire, fell on their faces to acknowledge the same and confess that - THE LORD – HE IS GOD!

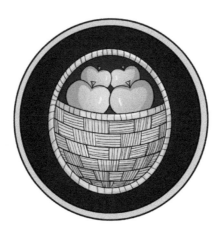

# Chapter 8
# There is a Place

# THEY HAVE SOMETHING TO GIVE

They have something to give
something to offer
Only if you play their tune
and sing their song
They have rewards, great rewards
for all who walk their way

Has not the Master of our souls
a reward to give?
Did He not promise us that which
the world cannot give?

Without faith it is impossible to please Him
for he that comes to God
must believe that He is
and He is a rewarder of them
who diligently seek Him
(*Hebrews 12:6*)

He gives rewards too you know
He bestows honour
which the devil both acknowledges and respects

The lions could not harm Daniel
jealous brothers could not destroy Joseph
Shadrack, Meshak and Abednego
were not destroyed by fire
and Steven though murdered with stones
was honoured when his murderers
saw his face shine like an angel

He gives rewards like no one ever could
to those who follow Him
play His tune
and sing His songs
He writes their names in the Lamb's Book of Life!

Do you want an award?
A recognition that lasts through all eternity?
Follow the Lamb of God.
Play and dance to His tune
sing His songs
His rewards are not fleeting memories
nor ornaments that can get lost or be destroyed
He gives always what the world cannot give

# COULD YOU WIN?

And could you win
in our world of need?
The bell of chance rings
the chance is uncertain as chance always is
The phrase they use is always the same
and you could win.

Could you win?
Everything is about taking a chance
a chance that could make you rich
a chance that could make you lose the little you have
It could be you, they say
As week after week
month after month
it never is you
but still the chance remains
It could be you!
Could you win?

Yet in this same world the old, old message
 rings true always
tested and tried for centuries on end
for God so loved the world
that he gave his only begotten son
that whosoever believes in him
should not perish
but HAVE ETERNAL LIFE!
It is not chance with Jesus Christ
There is no uncertainty here!

He does not put our names in a hat,
mix them up and ask the angels to pick one or two
With Jesus the message is not that it could be you
It is clear and true that it is you!

Yes, He died for you!
Put your hand in his today
and you will not have to wait for eternity
to find out if your number has come up!
Here and now, today!

You can know him in your heart and in your soul
eternally!
When you ask him to come in he comes in
 Jesus of Nazareth!
He says 'I stand at the door and knock
 if any man hears my voice
and opens the door
 I WILL come in! (Rev 3:20)

There are no chances with Jesus
What he says is what it is!
AMEN.

# KNOW YOUR BEARINGS

Those little annoying things which easily trip you up
or make you slip into that hole of irritability
Those periods in life when you jump to conclusions
and answer questions before you hear them
That long distant hurtful memory
that comes to the fore to make you think
that you know what people are thinking
or what they might do
These are landmarks to make you know your bearings

If they are not identified to be what they are
they will keep tripping you
until you become a difficult person
to live and work with

When you become irritable
and less tolerant with people
stop and check your bearings
lest irritability and intolerance become your nature

Let it not be known and said of you
'That is how she/he is'

The mercy and the grace of God
changes us from what we are
 to what He would have us to be

We all need to take time out and take stock.
The only checklist we have is *Galatians 5:22*

Peace and grace are wonderful soul mates
they cannot be bought, acquired or inherited
God's Holy Spirit bears this fruit in us
only when we are willing to allow Him to
when we know our bearings
and appreciate those things that trip us up

# FORGIVE YOURSELF

You thought you were right
when you were blind to the needs of others
You said and did things you thought were right
Now you know you were wrong
Someone is bruised by what you said
someone is hurt by what you did
You are sorry for it all
God forgives those who repent
so forgive yourself
Learn from the past and move on
All men have sinned
and come short of the glory of God
That includes <u>YOU.</u>
Accept his forgiveness
Forgive Yourself.

# THEY ARE CALLED KIND PEOPLE

There are many who walk the earth
There are many who rule
There are many who live with pain
sorrow and shattered dreams
Among them there are those who have been
put on this earth to make things brighter
They have known their own sorrows
their own pain, disappointments and shattered dreams

But they have chosen to offer themselves to others for
comfort
They live in every kingdom
They have no race, colour or class
No recognized status
Their names never make it to the front pages
neither will their photographs be on the cover of
magazines

They have a rare beauty
which is not readily visible to human eyes
except when that gentle smile in their eyes
invites and welcomes those seeking comfort
They communicate warmth without saying much
Their time they freely give
Something deep inside responds to their touch
They are called kind people
Poor is the community who does not have them
Sad is anybody that never meets them

Every nation, every people, every language needs them
They lighten burdens
help us to see the brighter side of life
In their presence is a place we can call home
It is only when we meet them
that we seek to be like them
to provide comfort to others in need
They are kind, not for reward
nor yet for recognition
Kindness has become second nature to them
It is just the way they are

Blessed are those who meet them
but more blessed are those
who meet the one who made them so

# INTEGRITY

Integrity is a costly garment worn by some rulers and kings. It is designed for leaders in society and those who are privileged to be taught its worth. Integrity shines forth not in words but in character, in the very being of the person it owns.

Integrity is costly but it cannot be bought. Yet if it is allowed a place in a person's life it takes over the very soul and sets that person apart. It is the only costly garment that may be worn by the poorest of men, and the greatest honour conferred on the weakest.

Integrity is beautiful and provides safety in the strangest of places. Many do not know its worth and sadly cast it away, yet it may be picked up by those who are clever at heart, though they may appear less equipped in mind. Integrity, like the salt of the earth, is what nations and communities are built on.

A person of integrity is true to his own soul. He does not brush aside, nor treat with contempt, those who he may perceive as being of less worth than himself.

Integrity is what makes the world go round. The earth has been drenched with the blood of men and women who have refused to compromise the truth they know. They say what they mean, and mean what they say. To have the courage of your convictions and to stand for what you believe crowns many with strength of character: the integrity which permeates our everyday lives and brings lasting beauty to our relationships.

Integrity costs a lot because it makes demands on every aspect of your life. To be true to yourself helps you to be true to others.

In every culture and tradition, men and women of integrity hold their communities together. They see wrong for what it is, even if it is dressed up and paraded as right. They know falsehoods even when it is glossed over with the paint of truth. They may not be in a hurry to expose wrong, but they work to help those who are willing to see the errors of their ways. Their silence does not condone falsehood, but they wait for the appropriate time to strip the paint and reveal the deception beneath it.

Integrity is a costly garment, but it can be owned by the poorest of men. It is taught deep in the recesses of the soul to all whose desire is to uphold the right and true.

# FIND YOUR WAY THROUGH THE CROWD

Find your way through the crowd
Someone is waiting for you at the other end
Her joy is worth every effort you made when
 you wrote a poem exclusively for her
Find your way through the crowd

They do not know and may not appreciate
your rhyme or reason
until you reach your target
the one for whom the poem was written

Her joy electrifies the crowd
She screams out your name
and now everybody is looking at you
because you wrote a poem
exclusively for one person.

# THERE IS A PLACE

There is a place where truth dwells.
There we can say we were wrong. There we can ask for forgiveness and receive pardon in the place where truth dwells.
There is a place where light dwells. There we can see what we only imagined or assumed. There we can clean the cobwebs and the dust which covered our minds in the dark.
If we are willing to stand in the place of truth, we cease to make excuses. We plant no devices or manufacture anything bearing no resemblance to the truth. In the light everything is revealed, yet we hide truth in empty boxes and cover our shame with hollow words.
What does it profit us when we go to lengths to manufacture things that are not true? What is it that burns within to make us find what is not there, just to cover our shame of being wrong?
Can't we say we are wrong in the face of truth? What a different world this would be if we could say we were wrong, and how beautiful it would be when truth sheds more light to prove us right. Truth: not manufactured, not manipulated, not fabricated. This beautiful wholesome truth always reveals to us that we are frail and human.
What a shame when the truth we hide for many years finally catches up with us. What a shame for men of renown to face prison sentences in their old age for refusing to acknowledge truth. Truth has a way of surfacing no matter how deep it has been buried.

# HELP IN TIME OF NEED

To be like our master
To be changed into his image
He saw need everywhere
and stepped in to help
We have a record of the ten lepers
Only one returned to say "thank you"
So it is sometimes
those we have helped forget what we have done
but we want to be like our master
To be changed into his image

He did not always wait to be asked
The five thousand never said they were hungry
The widow who lost her only son never asked for him to
be raised
Compassion is the nature of our lord
so he stopped to help without being asked
To be like our master
To be changed into his image

The disciples were fishing all night
They caught nothing
He stood out by the shore in the morning
telling them what to do
when they brought their catch ashore
Breakfast was ready
Jesus would cook for anyone who has worked all night
and is tired
To be like our master
To be changed into his image

He helped the thankful and the thankless
He went into homes where the people were ready to
receive Him
But did not give hospitality
Nobody washed his feet as was the custom
No oil was poured on his head as an honoured guest
yet he sat and ate with them
until a woman of the street came in
to wash his feet with tears of repentance
and dry them with her hair
She brought the most expensive thing she owned
and anointed his head with her oil
Sometimes we will receive kindness
in return for what we do
Sometimes our needs are ignored by those
who should know better
In it all we want to be like our master
To be changed into his image

Not to wait to be asked to help in time of need
Not to feel hurt when we are taken for granted

# HE CALLS TO US IN STRANGE PLACES

He comes to us in strange places, doing strange things
like walking on the water in the middle of the night.
He comes when he is least expected; in a time of trouble
when the winds of life blow against us.
He does not mean to frighten us, even when it seems as
if our situation has gone from bad to worse. Battling
against the wind in the middle of the night is bad enough
without seeing a ghost floating as it were on the water.
Why did he choose to come that way?
Is it to show us that He will come to us whichever way
he chooses? Is it to show us that He must not be put in a
box, expecting Him to act in a way to suit us? His ways
cannot be predicted! (Isaiah 55:8-9)
He is not an actor to perform in a lead role or be part of
the cast. He is Sovereign Lord in all His ways.
We must learn to accept Him to be who He is; Lord and
Master, never a puppet to do as we please.
Then it won't matter which way He comes to us
because in our fright we will hear Him say
'It is I do not be afraid' (Matt 14:27)

# PRESS ON, PRESS ON

Press on, press on
It is your duty to press on
No mountain will stand in your way
if you press on

Mountains and obstacles have respect
for those who press on
Mountains and obstacles can be conquered
by those who press on
and you will be a conqueror when you press on
for that is what He called us to be

Over-comers and more-than-conquerors
That is what we must be
So press on, press on
It is your duty for today
and your joy through life
to simply press on

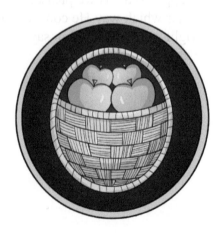

# Chapter 9
# This is My King

# I CAN TRUST GOD

He knows all things. If I cannot trust any man to be truthful in their dealings with me, I can trust God to reveal His truth and compassion to them. When men bend the truth to suit their purposes, I know the eternal Judge sees and hears every secret thought, word and deed.

No meeting, text message, email or telephone call disguising a lie as the truth is hidden from Him. He is my righteous judge and defence in every little detail of my life.

One day we shall all appear before Him, whether we believe in him or not. This is my strength and will always be, because I know that He alone brings justice when men think they have got away with the wrongs they have done.

# NEVER FAR AWAY

In times of need, dear Lord, You have never been far away. Oh how you have provided. It is only You, dear Lord, day by day, who has increased my strength. Your ways, sweet Lord, are past understanding. You will surely have a way in this also for me.

Help me not to bear a grudge. Help me not to seek to be understood. Help me not to be angry or hurt or bitter. Send your healing sunshine into my soul. Give me grace, dear Lord; grace to be graceful even in this difficult situation.

# I CAN DO ALL THINGS THROUGH CHRIST

I can
I can if I but take one day at a time
if I rely on His strength alone
if I resign from the world and go with Him
step by step
day by day
moment by moment
for He alone will see me through
He alone knows His plans
He has the timetable
and he holds the keys
When the going is hard
let me say "YES I CAN"
for in Him all things are possible
In Him we climb insurmountable hills

Yes, I can do all things through Christ
who strengthens me (Phil 4:13)

# THIS IS MY KING

This is my King. This is my Hero. This is my Lord and my saviour. He is King of Kings and Lord of Lords. He that was despised and forsaken. Rejected of men, unwanted, thrown away. Nailed to the cross: Mocked, spat upon, scourged, yet He opened out His mouth: He was led as a lamb to the slaughter. To those who mocked Him, He was a fool. They made fun of Him and laughed Him to scorn, called Him names and pushed Him about. Yet my God, my King, and the lover of my soul, opened not his mouth. His battle was to be silent.

His ammunition was to be compassionate, even to them that nailed Him to the cross. Yes, He opened not his mouth. Can we go all the way with Him? Can I take His hand and go with Him? He calls for me, His hand stretched out. But I am so afraid, so touchy, so scared. I yearn to be loved, to be accepted and be understood.

Yet here stands my Hero: despised, rejected, a man of sorrow and acquainted with grief. Misunderstood, called a devil and mad man.

Lily of the valley, fairest of ten thousand; Rose of Sharon; Bright and morning star; King of Kings and Lord of Lords.

And He says "Come with me my dear. I know how it feels- I've been there- but I can carry you through."

# HE IS SO HIGH

He made all things by the word of mouth
From the dust of the ground he made man
He is worshipped and adored by a host of angels
day and night
yet He seeks friendship with man

He is called the friend of Abraham
When His son took on human flesh
he made friends with tax collectors and sinners
He called his disciples friends

Today He is still calling out to all who value friendship
to come and be His friends
To be a friend of Jesus
is to have the best friend in heaven and on earth

He is always there when I call
promises never to leave nor forsake
and though I am not the best friend he's ever had
He makes me feel special
for He died on the cross for me
and rose again to give me eternal life

# THE FIRST DAY OF THE WEEK

This joy must rule my life every day
The joy of the first day of the week
when everything changed
The stone was rolled away from the tomb
The darkness that covered the understanding
of the disciples was lifted
The fear which kept them behind closed doors departed
A new day had come to every man, woman and child
The old order had changed.
The threat of crucifixion
no longer silenced those who believed in him
There was no longer anything in all creation
that will be able to separate us
from the love of God in Christ Jesus.
What a joy in knowing
that there is nothing to hold me down any more
because not only has He risen from the dead
He holds the keys of death and hell.

# I NEED TO SAIL THIS OCEAN TO MY DESTINATION

This is but a journey, many have travelled before me.
I may even count myself honoured to know something
of what countless numbers have suffered and endured.
There are songs, stories and art left behind by those who
have known what this ocean of life lashes out and foams
up.

They have known what it means to be tossed about on
rough seas. They wrote their experiences in songs,
stories and in art. Why does it feel that somehow I could
be alone in this? Am I not just another person sailing on
this tempestuous ocean? In this storm I choose to
remember calm waters on a moonlit night, when the
ocean was peaceful and I was glad to be a sailor.

I remember the dawn when the stars said their goodbyes
one by one as the sky lent itself to the paint brush of the
morning sun.

I remember the calm days of warm sunshine making the
sea blue and clear. I could see the fish swimming along
my boat as if drawn by some curiosity. I was glad then
to be a sailor.

Now the sea is rough and angry. The storm seems to have quarrelled with someone it once loved. It is angry, furious and I am caught in the middle of it all.

The sea is not angry at me. Why should it be? I have said nothing to the wind so it can't have been me that made it angry. Yet I travel on an angry ocean; no sun, no moon, no stars. I wonder where all the fish have gone. Still I must sail on this ocean till I reach my destination.

The sea is angry so I must keep my cool. The wind blows me about in all directions so I must keep still. How can I fight the ocean? What do I say to the wind? Peace! Be Still?

I know of a man whose voice the winds and the waves obey. I will make my supplications to Him, and write a few poems for those who will sail this ocean.

# PSALM 46 (THIS IS WHERE I WANT TO RUN TO)

*'Therefore we will not fear'*

Learning not to fear without knowing God as our refuge is like trying to climb a dangerous mountain without a harness or walking a tightrope with no safety net.

There are situations in life that make us feel that the very earth we walk on has been removed from under our feet. When disaster strikes most people will reach out to Plan B.

When all our plans collapse and there is nothing visible in sight that could give us a glimmer of hope, it would be insane for us to think we could stand or survive without faith in God.

There are many who have jumped into the sea and drowned because the mountains they looked up to were also thrown into the sea.

This psalm describes the worst situations which could happen to any of us.

The Psalmist started by telling us the reason why we will not fear.

He spoke about the only reason why some people could survive physical, emotional, financial, spiritual and psychological trauma. And there is only one reason.

We know without a doubt that God is our refuge and strength. This knowledge has come through our relationship with Him, our daily communion and friendship with Him, through reading, meditating and listening to His word. We have been brought to a place where doubt has been banished from our hearts and minds.

We know He is very <u>present</u> all the time even in times of trouble. I believe that presence means I do not have to scream out to Him for help. It means that He is right by my side when all have deserted me. It means that He has not left and will never leave when the closest of my relations leave me.

When I am blamed, accused for some wrong so bad that no one wants to be associated with me; the One who knows the truth; the One who cannot be manipulated by lies; the One whose opinion cannot be swayed and whose integrity cannot be tarnished stands close by me. The One before whom I can be still and know that His position as God will never change!

# YOU TOOK ALL MY SHAME AWAY

You took all my shame away
You took the disgrace
You allowed me to have a face
You gave me a voice

That is why you came
to open the door to freedom
when men had put labels on me
when I became a byword

You reached out and touched me
You took away my shame
Nobody ever suffered shame the way you did
spat on and mocked, jeered and condemned

You took my place when you
carried the cross of shame
when even the closest friend denied
ever knowing you.

You were alone in your grief
They all fell asleep in your time of need.
Where were all your friends?
Where were those who cried
Hosanna when you had something to give?

Some stayed far off
Some stayed behind closed doors
Except the woman who bore you and
the disciple you loved

160

None understood what it was all about
Even the centurion who had a revelation
of who you were did not understand
that it was for me you died that cruel death

The precious blood which flowed from your head,
hands and feet, covered time and eternity
It covered my sin and shame
It is available today in the same
freshness and power as it did
the day it was poured out for me

I do not have to stay behind closed doors any more
I do not have to look over my shoulder
I do not have to cover my face and wish
for the earth to open up and swallow me

You took away my shame
When men mocked and said what they liked
Men may still try and stick labels on me

They do not know, they may
not have heard as yet
that you took all my shame
every disgrace which belonged to me.

You have turned every failure into success
and success is living in freedom from fear and shame.

# SURELY HE MUST HAVE A PURPOSE IN ALL THESE THINGS

Make me strong
Surely He must have a purpose in all these things
for nothing happens by chance to the child of God
Yes, there must be a purpose in this, also for me
Dear Lord, help me to wait, help me to be still
Help me to work when I can't find my way
All my strength comes from thee
for except you build the house
they labour in vain that build it. Ps127:1
Build my house and my home oh Lord
Be with us
Give me the strength I need
for every task that is mine to perform
Make me strong, my Lord and my God

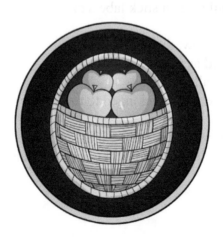

# Chapter 10
## A Tale That is Told

# WHEN NOT BEING ENGLISH

When not being English and you try to write in English
your handicap of not being English may entertain
Be glad it is so
for the English will probably appreciate your effort
and may even like what may not sound so English.
They may fall in love with your mind and forgive you
then perhaps not being English
won't be such a handicap to communication
as you feared
Soon, being English
or not being English
will not hinder your attempt to write

*(I decided not to let 'not being English' prevent me from
writing. I am grateful to my friends who have
encouraged me over the years, and would like to express
my special thanks and appreciation to Mrs. Deanne
Morgan and Mrs. Linda Williams.)*

# A LITTLE FLOWER POT

This hall is so large
I feel almost invisible in it
There are so many people, great and small, tall and short
Everyone has something to give
Bright colours, dull colours
paints and pencils to design and create

All I brought is a little flower pot, and it is empty
I stand it on this shelf and wait
I hear someone brought seeds that will grow
Another person has some water
We all brought something
so please don't drive me away
because all I brought is a little flower pot

Fill it with compost, let's sow the seeds
Pour on it some water, let's watch them grow
Whatever you brought, please don't go away
When we see the colour burst forth
and smell the fragrance it brings
won't we be glad that we all brought something
which grew in a little flower pot?

*I wrote* A Little Flower Pot *to express how I felt at the awards ceremony in Washington DC – after years of just writing poems and filing them away, it was good to meet with many poets from all over the world. Listening to other peoples' poetry made me feel that my work represented a little flower pot. The inspiration I received from friends and the encouragement I received from family was what I would describe as "compost and water". The seeds are the original ideas, which, through the help of friends and family, have bloomed in an explosion of colour.*

# THIS IS WHAT YOU GET

This is what you get
when you have a poet for a wife
She sees a line in all you do
and writes them down before you look

Your meals are cooked
(well, most of the time)
and when you help around the house
she gets the time to click the mouse

Too busy she may be, but never unkind
She feels your need for warmth as only poets do
She gives, she takes, and it is all about love
And what is left over, she puts in a verse

Computers and word processors
will never take your place
They all just come in handy
when she has too much to give.

She knows you get tired
She allows you to sleep
as she lies awake thinking
of the news of the week
She tip toes down stairs
and turns on the light to write down her thoughts
before they are all robbed by sleep.

You reach for her in bed,
her place is empty.
You wonder where she's gone
at two o'clock in the morning.

You call out to her
She is sitting by the desk
This is what you get
when you have a poet for a wife.

# IF THE WORLD IS A STAGE

If the world is a stage, and all men and women are
merely players
if life is but their exits and entrances
then my life on the stage of life must be
what the script says it must be!
Shakespeare did not tell of the script and who wrote it
neither did he tell us who the stage managers are
nor who the critics might be
The world, a great big stage indeed!
And since all men and women are merely players
there cannot be much of an audience
Yet depending on the script played
the impact, influence and interest remain
for generations unborn

As it is with Shakespeare
his stage direction was to write scripts for others to play
so long after he bowed and left the stage
His script remains
and I think that somehow we all leave something behind
which is passed on to generations unborn
whether they be traditions, values or memories
handed down either in script or word of mouth
these remain if only to say
once upon a time
there was a person with such and such a name
So the world may be a stage with a script
written before we made our entrance

# A TALE THAT IS TOLD

We live our lives as a tale that is told. Eternity is only a second away. In a moment, in the twinkling of an eye we are absent from the body and present with the Lord. Though we are mourned by the few or many we leave behind, we become a memory to those who were dear to us and a name to the rest.

On this side it is all over, a book closed, the last page read. Its pages opened only occasionally in the memory. Here on earth prayers are said, candles lit, flowers lain and tears if any shed.

How different things are on the other side: the contrasting peace, joy and love in the presence of the Lord, for that is what He promised. The saints worship day and night, except there is no night.

How very different heaven must be; to experience no pain, no worry, no fears. Finally we accomplish the purpose for which we were made, to worship God in holiness.

We live our lives as a tale that is told, yet how often do we pause to think of that other place which has awaited us since the day we were born? Born to live on earth, appreciate its beauty and work to preserve it so it may continue to nurture all of us, even those yet unborn, to love and be loved, to care for each other until we are called to the other side.

Grant us the grace, good Lord, to live in the transient and temporal while looking forward to life eternal and full of glory freely offered to whosoever will accept by Jesus of Nazareth.

# SERVANT GIRL

Don't listen to what they say
Know me for yourself
The hired men have done their best
and spread rumours around the nest
of who I never was nor ever will be
So don't listen to what they say
Know me for yourself
Those robes they made for me
are not meant to be worn by those who wear crowns
They walk on marble
and eat their meals in a golden dish
You can see I walk on dusty ground
I drink no wine
my water is from a calabash
The purple robe is nice, I know
It reaches down to my toes
Soft shoes of leather, I admire
my flip flops are good enough
So when they call me Queen
Do not believe it
I am only a servant girl
Privileged to serve the King of Kings
whose assignment for me is serving others
He hides in all the people I meet
of every class and clan, race and status
My king lives in them all
And he says, whatever you do for them you do for me
This is why I can never become Queen
even though you make a purple robe for me.

# HE TOOK AWAY THE KEYS

He took away the keys. "Do you call me Master?" He asked.

"Yes Lord" I replied.

He looked at me intently, with love and with pity.  He yearned beyond words to run my life, but I clutched the keys in my hand. I knew very well that at my very best I made a mess of life, yet I held onto the keys as though I could make things better.

He will not force me to surrender. That is not His way. If He was Master, as the look in His eyes conveyed, then He had a right over my life. Reluctantly I handed the keys to Him. Suddenly my life took a new turn. Fear disappeared, so did anxiety. The joy and comfort of knowing someone else was in charge, whatever happens. The rest he provided to prove why I was foolish for so long, clutching the keys of my life so tightly.

# WHY DID I PANIC?

Why did I panic? Lord, why did I panic?
You promised never to leave me nor forsake me
Yet why did I panic Lord, why did I panic?
Why did I panic at the fury of the oppressor?
You promised in Your word
that Your presence will go with me
and You will give me peace,
yet why did I panic, Lord, why did I panic?

Why did I allow fear to be part of our sacred company?
How was fear able to travel along with You by my side?
How could the lying tongues and intimidation
find a way to steal my joy
while your promise never to leave nor forsake
holds true for time and eternity?

Forgive me Lord
for allowing Your joy which is my strength
to be stolen

Forgive me, Lord
for focusing on the intimidation of the enemy
rather than on your presence with me.

Forgive me
for living as if the Son of the Most High God
was not my friend.
Why did I panic, Lord, why did I panic?
As though You were a man
who was not true to His word?

You are with me always
through every storm
and when the raging fires destroy all I can see
when friends disappoint
and the lies told about me
are held as though they were eternal truth

You are with me, Lord
You promised always to be near
to deliver, to vindicate
and lift up my head above my enemies and my foes

This is my privilege
this is my honour, my glory and my reason for living.
The creator of the whole universe is my friend.
Why should I panic?

# YOU LEAD ME

You lead me you lead me in ways that overwhelm me.
You lead me to the poor you lead me to the rich.
You lead me to those who hurt; you lead me to those
who mourn.
You lead me Lord you lead me
And when I have nothing much to say
 you help me listen till I can feel their pain.
I am humbled Lord that you would lead me to those
who need your touch, your peace and grace.

You know them, you feel their aching hearts, and you
 send me?
What can I say or do to ease their pain?
Just being there for your love to flow
Through this unworthy vessel that is me.
And I wonder why there is so much pain and hurt in our
world.
I do not wish to plan and do things my way any more
 Lord you overwhelm me.

When they come, those who come, it is not to me Lord,
 They come to you Lord, it is to you they come.
You have the words of eternal life.
You are the resurrection and life.
Help me to always remember that I have nothing
 of my own to set before them
Bread of life, light of the world,
Prince of peace it is to you they come.

It is a privilege to be in your service.

# YOU ARE HERE WITH ME LORD AND I AM NOT AFRAID

You are here with me Lord and I am not afraid. The children are asleep in Your arms and in Your arms I lay down to sleep also. Give us sleep and rest, oh Lord, and refresh us.

Be with Your servant Sam as he looks to You for strength. Be with him Lord and direct his thoughts and his ways. May this time be forever blessed Lord, as You strengthen us by Your presence alone.

Help us to draw closer to You. Help us to know You and love You more and more. And we want to say we love You Lord. For You are from everlasting to everlasting and we adore You Lord.

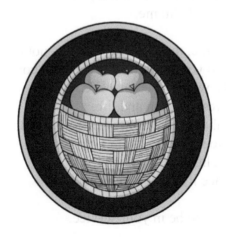

# AUTHOR PROFILE

Hannah Yaawusuah Adjepong was born and raised in Ghana, West Africa.

After leaving school she taught as a pupil teacher in two primary schools in the north of Ghana before gaining entrance into nursing school.

Qualifying first of all as a QRN (Qualified Registered Nurse), she worked at the Tamale Central and Yendi hospitals and later transferred to Effia Nkwanta hospital, Sekondi-Takoradi, where she became a State Registered Nurse.

It was during her time at Sekondi-Takoradi that Mrs. Adjepong ran a Sunday School for the children of doctors and nurses, who because of the nature of their work could not always take their families to church.

She also worked with the Child Evangelism Fellowship, Scripture Union, the Nurse's Christian Fellowship. She was a lay preacher at the local Presbyterian and Methodist churches, and was often invited to speak for the Anglican Women of Sekondi. Mrs. Adjepong's faith became interdenominational; she observes that "there is nothing more beautiful than when Christians of all denominations worship together."

As a Sunday school teacher, Mrs. Adjepong often had help from other Christians who offered ideas on drama and music. One such person was the young Dr. S. E. Adjepong, who played the guitar for the children as they sang beautiful songs and choruses. Their engagement came as no surprise, at least to the Sunday school children.

After their wedding Dr. and Mrs. Adjepong moved to the big city of Accra, where Dr. Adjepong began his postgraduate surgical training at the Korle-Bu Teaching Hospital.

Mrs. Adjepong wrote her first play *The Hands That Care* in 1979 and it was performed by members of the Nurses Christian Fellowship.

While training as a midwife, it was natural for the Adjepongs to start their own family. She laughs about it today when she calls it "practical midwifery".

Dr. Adjepong left his young family to complete his surgical training in the UK, and they joined him eight months later.

Raising four children under the age of seven meant that Mrs. Adjepong had to call on her past teaching experience to teach and entertain her growing family. No wonder her short stories and poetry came in handy.

"*The day the magicians went home without their magic wand*" was a story she devised for telling her children about Moses in Pharaoh's court.

Writing about Auntie Kotiah brought her childhood memories alive. "This gave us all a lot of fun, which is what most people need when raising children."

Working around her family as a part-time nurse with the elderly, she found time to continue writing poetry. Her work was given a special recognition when she received the International Poet of Merit Award in Washington DC, USA, September 1999.

She won three more International Poet of Merit Awards and received the title of Distinguished Poet in 2003.

Her speaking engagements earned her an invitation to work as a storyteller in primary schools, which led to the creation of Life Affirming Stories.

Some of her poetry is available to purchase on posters and greeting cards.

To view or purchase her books please visit www.hannahyaawusuahadjepong.co.uk

## Upcoming Poetry Books
## by Hannah Yaawusuah Adjepong

*Stranger in the Land*
*Solid Gold*
*Reflections*
*Fragments*
*Voice of Comfort*

#0002 - 021018 - C0 - 210/148/11 - PB - 9781909094154